90% Of
Lawn Care Businesses
Fail
In Their First Year.
Learn How To Survive
With These Tips!

**From The Gopher Lawn Care Business Forum &
The GopherHaul Lawn Care Business Show**

By Steve Low

Table of Contents

INTRODUCTION

Welcome.

Everyday you run your lawn care business, you are going to be coming into contact with new experiences, situations, and jobs that will change you. These experiences will also change the way you operate your business. Sometimes you will make it through a challenging situation unscathed, other times, you may find yourself just barely able to hold on. Some experiences can even be fatal to your lawn care business.

When 90% of new start up lawn care business owners fail in their first year, a need for information on how to survive is essential. You need as much education and early warning as you can get your hands on to make it through where others have failed.

This book's goal is to give you a heads up of what other lawn care business owners have experienced and how they dealt with their challenging situations. Learn from these insights and grow stronger because of them.

As the old saying goes 'those who fail to learn from history are doomed to repeat it.' Don't be doomed, read on entrepreneur, read on!

Until the next time we meet, always remember to Dream It, Build It, Gopher It!

Sincerely,

Steve

Special Thanks to Gopher Lawn Care Software.

This book would not have been possible without the help and guidance from all our friends and business owners we have met over the years on our Gopher Lawn Care Business Forum.

Also thank you to the staff at Gopher Software for making all of this happen.

Lawn Care Software

PROBLEM: Scheduling & billing repetitive jobs is tedious and time consuming.
SOLUTION: Gopher Billing & Scheduling Software allows you to Quickly and Easily schedule jobs and create invoices.

Gopher Landscape Billing and Scheduling Software simplifies the task of scheduling your lawn care jobs and billing your customers. Simply set up your jobs at the beginning of the season and let Gopher handle the rest. With Gopher, you can print out a list of scheduled jobs for each day and then automatically print invoices after those jobs have been completed.

Continue your reading.

I have more great information on running a lawn care business in my other books, **"Stop Lowballing! A Lawn Care Business Owner's Guide To Success."**

 Some of the topics discussed in the book: - How to start up your lawn care business. - Finding your niche and finding profits. - Lawn Care Equipment. - Pricing & Estimating Lawn Care Jobs. - Dealing With Customers. - Dealing With Employees. - Lawn Care Marketing Secrets. - Lawn Care Business Tips. - Getting Commercial Accounts without commercial references. - Pitfalls of Commercial Accounts. And more.

The GopherHaul Lawn Care Marketing & Landscaping Business Show Episode Guide. Topics discuss include: How to raise start up capital. Seasonal marketing ideas. What to do when your largest client leaves? What's better to use, postcards or brochures? How to build your customer base with referrals? Gain one customer then lose one customer. How to stop it? How to pre-qualify customers when they call? How to bid jobs. What should you include in a commercial lawn care bid? What newspaper ads work best? How to buy a lawn care business. Tips on buying used lawn care equipment. And much more.

How to get customers for your landscaping and lawn care business all year long. Volume 1.
Anyone can start a lawn care business, the tricky part is finding customers. Learn how in this book. New lawn care business owners were polled and 33% of them said the toughest part about running their business was finding customers. This book shows you how to get new lawn care customers. Don't start from scratch and try to re-create the wheel. Learn what works and what doesn't.

Volume #1 discusses: Getting started, choosing a business name, harnessing employees to sell, community marketing ideas, free rentals to offer, hosting events to get exposure, volunteer projects to build goodwill, how to get residential and commercial customers (including sample letters). Bikini lawn care, getting in your local paper, marketing on price, publicity stunts & media attention, organic lawn care marketing, reaching out to realtors, turning hobbies into marketing ideas, seasonal marketing ideas that work.

How to get customers for your landscaping and lawn care business all year long. Volume 2.

Volume #2 discusses: The most effective lawn care business marketing methods. How to track your ads, the best ways to utilize: billboards, brochures, business cards, buying lawn care customers, clubs & organizations, coupons & gift cards, co-marketing, door hangers, going door to door, flyers, internet marketing, lawn signs, customer letters, direct mailing, newsletters, newspaper ad, phone book advertising, phones & telemarketing, postcards, referrals, sports, testimonials, trade shows, truck & trailer advertising, word of mouth.

The Big Lawn Care Marketing Book
This book contains 470 pages of marketing ideas to help your lawn care & landscaping business grow.
The Big Lawn Care Marketing Book contains volume 1 & 2 of my other books "How to get customers for your landscaping and lawn care business all year long."

The landscaping and lawn care business plan startup guide.

If you ever had thought about starting your own lawn care or landscaping business but weren't sure how to go about putting together a business plan, this book will show you examples of lawn care business plans created on the Gopher Lawn Care Business Forum.

Inside is a step by step guide on how to make a landscape or lawn care business plan with real life examples including income and expense projections as well as customer acquisition goals. This lawn care business book is a great tool to help you improve your odds of finding success.

How to use Gopher Lawn Care Business Billing & Scheduling Software.

Learn how to manage your lawn care and landscaping business easier with this powerful software.

A Rebellious Teenagers Guide To Starting A Landscaping & Lawn Care Business.

When you are a teenager you have a lot of rebellious energy. Why not take that energy, harness it to be productive, and make money! This book will show you how to succeed in starting your own landscaping & lawn care business. I cover the basics of how to register your business to advanced topics like incentives to get employees to sell more.

GopherHaul Extreme Lawn Care Business Tips.

Unfiltered, unedited, and a little rough. A collection of landscaping & lawn care business lessons I've learned along the way.

I see so many new lawn care businesses get started only to fail a short time later because the entrepreneurs didn't educate themselves enough about their field. Here is a collection of lessons I learned that will give your lawn care or landscaping business a better chance at success.

Lawn Care Business Tips, Tricks, & Secrets From The Gopher Lawn Care Business Forum & The GopherHaul Lawn Care Business Show.
The vast majority of new lawn care businesses fail simply because they don't know the tips, tricks, and secrets veteran lawn care business owners have learned through years of trial and error. This book will share with you what you need to know.

The GopherHaul guide on how to get customers for your landscaping and lawn care business - Volume 3.
Coming up with marketing and service ideas to keep busy and profitable all year long can be difficult. Most of the times we are just not in the mood to sit and think up creative ways to make more money.
Well thankfully I have been able to interview thousands of lawn care business owners over the years and ask them what's worked and what hasn't. The responses and the follow up questions have really uncovered a treasure trove of ideas that I compiled here to share with you.
Now you don't have to get frustrated when trying to come up with new ideas. Just keep this book around as a reference. Some of these ideas might just work right off the shelf while others might need to be altered to fit your needs. Ultimately it's always better to have ideas on stand by just in case.
This book is the third in a series of lawn care business marketing books I have published and contains lawn care marketing ideas cherry picked from previous content I have written as well as new unpublished material.

How to Make More Money with your lawn care or landscaping business. From The Gopher Lawn Care Business Forum & The GopherHaul Lawn Care Business Show.

Learn how to make more money with your lawn care or landscaping business.

Making money with your lawn care or landscaping business can be a challenge even in the best of times but it gets even tougher when you are up against heavy competition.

This book will help teach you what successful lawn care & landscaping business owners are doing to not only survive but to make more money than their competitors.

It covers how to make more money on bidding. How to read your customer's body language to know when you are charging too much or not enough. Learn the steps you should be taking to win more bids and things you should never do when trying to win a lawn care bid.

You will also learn how to deal with picky customers, those that live out of state, those that like to cancel service without giving you enough warning, and help you figure out how much your customers are actually worth.

Learn how to make more money with your lawn care crew by knowing the ideal crew size from others who have experimented with many different setups.

Learn the best way to purchase equipment, which equipment to purchase and how to use it in order to make your business more profitable plus much much more.

How To Get Commercial Lawn Care And Snow Plow Customers.

I put this book together because I know it can be so very difficult for newer lawn care, landscaping, or snow plow business owners to find out how to gain commercial customers. Do you just go in and knock on doors? Do you send them letters? How should they be approached?

All too often when people try things, they experiment once and if it doesn't give them the results they are looking for, they give up and think they just lacked some magical quality others who are successful must have that they don't.

Well there are no magical qualities, there are just certain tips and tricks we have seen that work over the years being discussed on the Gopher Lawn Care Business Forum and these are the tips I want to share with you. I also included some letter templates you can use to send to customers to get on their bidding list, to use as a cover letter for your bid, and to thank them at the end of the season.

If you are unsure on how to price out commercial jobs, I even included some examples what others have bid on for various commercial jobs.

Gaining new lawn care or snow plowing customers shouldn't be this hidden secret skill. It should be made readily available to you so that you can grow your lawn care business as big as you want, based on your desire and not based on luck or chance.

As you read through this book, you will see variations of certain lawn care marketing methods pop up again and again. When you see that, it's because those methods being discussed work. The variations you see are little tweaks that lawn care business owners utilize to stand out from others. You can use them too, or take the basic skills you learn here and create your own tweaks to make them uniquely yours.

When you are finished reading this book, I hope you feel like you have a successful family member in the lawn care business that has shared with you a lifetime of what he has learned.

It has taken many years to compile all these insights and business lessons and there is no doubt in my mind, your lawn care and snow plowing business will grow because of it.

CUSTOMERS

Worst lawn care customer.

Everyone who runs a business has customers. Sometimes those customers are a delight to work with while other times they can be nightmares. Everyone seems to do alright handling the happy customers but it can be a serious challenge to handle a difficult customer. Depending on the choices you make, challenging customer situations can be turned around or they can go from bad to worse. A lawn care business owner shared with us a situation he finds himself in every once in a while with difficult customers. He also tells us, on the Gopher Lawn Care Business Forum, the best way he has found to resolve the them.

He shared "for me, the worst customer is the one that constantly reminds me about what great service they had gotten from their previous lawn care provider. Then they tell me they only paid for lawn maintenance and the guy would trim their hedges and clean their garden for free.

When these situations happen, the question you have to ask yourself is, why isn't that lawn care business servicing them anymore? From my point of view, it's one of a few reasons why:

a) They did too many additional services for free and it caused them to lose their business.

b) The customer was actually supposed to pay for the hedge trimming etc, but didn't, and considered the job to be free after the guy discontinued service to them.

c) The lawn care business owner did the job for free once. But he was then expected to do it again in the future along with other jobs for free and because he found himself in a bad spot and couldn't say no, he ultimately discontinued servicing the customer.

In the past I might have been more willing to do extra side jobs for free but now I have to think to myself. Is it something simple like taking a small pile of debris? If so, I just throw it in the truck no problem. It also depends on what the customer is like. If I find the customer to be a pain in the butt and they tend to be late on paying their bill, even for small jobs I say 'I would have to charge you for that, would you like an estimate?'

For bigger time consuming jobs like hedge trimming and garden cleaning here is how I handle it.

Customer: The guy I used to have cut my lawn did my hedges and once in a while he'd clean out my garden for me for free, can you do that?

Me: I can absolutely help you with those additional services, but I will have to charge for them. Expenses like gas, wear and tear on my equipment, insurance, and my time can really catch up to me as a small business owner. Because I plan on being here for the long haul to serve you, I need to make sure I have those expenses covered.

You would be amazed at what people ask me to do for free. Through my advertising, I had two potential customers call me and ask for me to mow their lawn once for free, to see if it was worth it for them to hire me. I laughed so hard and told them it doesn't work that way, sorry.

Don't be a push over. Be nice, be helpful, be courteous, but always remember time is money and you need to make a profit or you won't be in business for long."

The downsides to buying a landscaping business.

Starting a landscaping business from scratch can be a real pain in the butt. If you are starting from nothing, it can seem like forever until you get a decent amount of customers. So maybe you have considered buying an existing landscaping business. What could go wrong though? What things do you need to keep an eye out for?

Well I got a chance to talk with a retired police officer who decided to buy an existing landscaping business and he shared some of the big issues he had to deal with on the Gopher Lawn Care Business Forum. It wasn't easy as he thought it would be. The existing business came along with existing problems he was initially unaware of and as he continues to investigate, he finds more.

He wrote "I have been running my own lawn care business now for the last two years. I am a retired police officer who sadly left the force after 14 year due to health problems and now I'm having a fantastic time running my own company but it didn't come easy or cheaply.

Things had been slow going at first and in order to grow my business I decided to look about for a landscaping company to buy and merge into my own. So about 10 days ago, I purchased a small existing landscaping business. I did it on the suggestion of a business broker who had been guiding me on a purchase of another business, which fell through. He said that the landscaping industry is very steady and gave a good opportunity to grow. I know nothing about landscaping as I had only focused on mowing thus far so I have my work cut out.

With the business purchase, I've inherited a three-man crew, pickup, three trailers and all the equipment necessary. The seller is helping me get up to speed. The foreman of the crew has been servicing the area for nine years and knows the homeowners very well. So well, in fact, that within a few days, I had already caught him taking money from them for 'extra services' and identified a couple of phantom customers (homeowners) who didn't appear on the list provided by the seller, yet the foreman had been serving and collecting money from.

Before trying to grow the biz, I figure that I have to learn it first, and consolidate the clients that I have. The most immediate problem seems to be scheduling. The seller has his own scheduling system that was a disaster. It basically was a combination of Word files that he updates to do the scheduling. It seems very confusing and relies mightily on personally knowing each and every customer and their yard.

As the season heats up, everything seems to grow faster and I am having a very difficult time trying to keep up. It also seems that every other truck on the road here is a landscaping company. Sure homeowners in my area spend millions and millions of dollars on this industry so I know there is plenty of money to be made. However right now I'm just trying to figure how to handle it all before it implodes.

My advice to you is grow slow and be wary about taking on more than you can chew. Oh and one last thing, customers you find on your own are going to be a lot more loyal than those you buy. This goes for employees too. So if you feel in the rush for growth, try marketing yourself more, before you look to buy an existing and more likely than not, problematic business."

Lawn care customers trying to take advantage of you?

As you run your lawn care business you will find the vast majority of lawn care customers to be happy with the service you offer and content enough to leave you to do your work. However there always will be a small percentage of them who will play games with you from the moment you meet. How you handle such problem customers can greatly effect your mood and your views on your business. If problem customers are allowed to continue to get under your skin, they may cause you to close shop in order to regain your sanity. This is a discussion that appeared on the Gopher Lawn Care Business Forum.

A lawn care business owner wrote "I have a couple of lawn care customers where seemingly everything I do is wrong and overpriced (and I'm WELL under the $60/hour rate). I believe they are trying to dupe me into performing more work for free by complaining about how much I charge (which we both agree upon prior to work commencing).

Today marks the 2nd time in the same week that a few customers have called to try and have me come back and do more work for no charge. So I'm now going to take down banana trees for free because my hedge trim job was not to their standard. I am really pissed I agreed to this.

Initially this one customer told me that they lost their previous lawn care guy and said he wouldn't return their calls. Now I know why. Nothing is ever good enough for them, and they are constantly complaining about being overcharged.

Has anyone else run into such problem customers? What have you done with customers like these? I really think I should do this last job and drop them because I can see that they'll be more trouble in the long run than they are worth. At the same time, I want positive word-of-mouth. I don't want them to run to their friends and say that my company is incompetent and expensive."

In such a situation, you can't let your fear of a single problem customer, bad mouthing you to their friends, stop you from moving on to greener pastures. Here is what a few other business owners shared.

- "If you can honestly say the job was done right and the price was prearranged and they continue with their bad behavior, drop them and move on. There are a few people like this out there and you are bound to pick one up every now and then. Once I dropped them I would replace them with someone who appreciates your hard work and approves of your prices."

- "Don't worry about bad word of mouth from him. He is a 'user' and everyone he knows, knows it. He is the type that is always trying to get someone to do something for him and never return the favor. He is the one that is always borrowing something and never returns it. His neighbors are probably wondering why you lasted so long!

Trying to satisfy him (who can't be satisfied) only takes time away from other customers. Drop him. He is not worth the aggravation."

- "I have two customers like this and they drive me insane. One just told me last week, when they received their bill, that I had not serviced their property all month! I had to kindly remind them that I was there as I had to pick up their previous month's payment 2 weeks late!

I plan on finishing out the month with them and then givin' em the boot."

- "All I can say, is drop them. PERIOD. Don't worry about the bad press from them. There are so many more client's out there. If a customer gives me a hard time and I did the job right and felt good about it, then strike 1. Next complaint, strike 2. The last issue, I tell them, they're Fired. I stand by my work 100%, and have customer telling me all the time how pleased they are with my service.

I am not about to let some bad apple customer ruin my day, week or month because they can't be satisfied. I started my business to enjoy myself and my life and to get away from people like that."

Don't let a lawn care customer go long without paying.

For many new lawn care business owners, there is this tendency to be a wishful thinker. If a lawn care customer owes you for one month's worth of work already, you might find that you try to justify in your head if you keep working, they will eventually pay you. You may also be afraid to stop work, because as a new business owner, you most likely need all the money you can get. This behavior takes you into a dangerous area where you most likely will get burned.

If you find yourself dealing with a few situations like this in a row, it may push you to a breaking point where you throw your hands up in the air and simply give up. Here is a story that talks about dealing with a difficult customer, from the Gopher Lawn Care Business Forum. Use this story to help gain foresight and see why you don't want to repeat this same situation in your business.

A lawn care business owner wrote "I have a lawn care customer that signed up for annual service with monthly billing in March. He owns a large corner lot with a lot of plant beds, shrubs, and trees. Our agreement was $100/month to include mowing, line trimming, edging, blow off, and then trimming and pruning of all bushes and trees under 15′ in height. Weed control was not included as the client handled that himself. In mid June the client was going away for a couple months and asked me if he could leave out some spray and a sprayer so I could spray the weeds for him? He said I could charge him extra if need be. I said no, I would spray for him and that there would be no extra charge, it's not a big deal.

Between June 25th & Sept 25th in addition to our regular work I treated the beds with his supplied chemical and sprayer on 5 or 6 occasions. After using the gallon he had mixed I noticed it wasn't working very well. When I went to mix gallon #2 I found the label on the bottle of concentrate was not legible as it was left outside. I called the client by phone and explained that it wasn't working very well and that I didn't know the proper mix for this off-brand product. He wasn't sure what the mix rate was off hand either and said 'I just mix some in water.' So I did the same, but it didn't kill anything. Next I tried again and upped the dosage with no change in results. So slowly the weeds overtook the beds, despite the spray (mind you I've called him about this already).

When the client returned to town around the week of Oct. 1st, He comments then that the weeds are out of control. I said 'I know, that's why I called you, the spray you supplied wasn't working!' So after that conversation, he goes and spends time out in the yard pulling all the weeds manually. There were times I was there mowing, trimming, and pruning while he was outside and he said nothing that would lead me to believe he was mad at me.

In December I call the client because he owes me for the months of October & November ($200). At that point, he tells me how he feels that I am responsible for the fact that the weeds got out of hand and he is pissed about it. He tells me he wants to cancel our agreement on the lawn and bushes (because of weed control that wasn't included. I sprayed them for a couple months with his stuff as a courtesy). The kicker to this all is the client refuses to pay the $200 he rightfully owes for the services rendered (that were actually in our agreement!) during the months of Oct. & Nov. He goes on to tell me how he spent 5 full days and had to get his cousin to help him for 3 more days pulling the weeds and that he feels this labor more than eats up the $200 in question.

I feel like it was a courtesy to spray, I didn't charge him and on top of that, he was NOTIFIED that it WASN'T WORKING. He feels that despite the lack of charge, I agreed to 'take care of the weeds' and had I not agreed he would have found someone who would have to done it in his absence. But since I said I'd spray, that it's all my responsibility and I should have pulled all the weeds or had my men do it.

The bottom line to me seems to be that the spray didn't work for me. He says it works. I don't know how thick he mixes it because I still don't even know what the proper mix is!? The label was destroyed and when I called, he didn't know either? It was not a product I am familiar with. (I don't even carry weed killer as I am not certified to do so. Though legally- if a customer supplies both chemical and application equipment it falls under a 'yardman exemption' and I can apply weed killer that way). I suppose I could have tracked down who sells that crap, got in the car, gone to the place and read a label on their bottle but hell? This was a courtesy thing after all.

The whole situation is frustrating as hell, I can tell you that. The part that makes it suck even more is that during the last month (which he is refusing to pay for) I spent hours and hours there doing a full fall clean up and trimmed everything on the property! This was included in the monthly rate but still that's assuming that I get paid. So everything is freshly trimmed for the winter and now he's gonna try to skip out of paying me for October and November on top of canceling a $100/month agreement going into the slower months….. agh! I bet he'll probably let the place go completely to hell until March and then hire some other poor schmuck for next season."

Another lawn care business owner suggested "it sounds like you are at one of those crossroads where you wonder if it is worth attempting to salvage this customer or just dump him and spend your time gaining other clients.

Here is what I have done in situations like this. Tell him your position once more just like you told us above and let him know that you truly feel like you handled the application of the chemical to the best of your ability. Let him know that you continued to maintain his lawn according to your contract and that you feel you should be paid in full for the duration of the contract.

Now comes the hard part. Once you feel he has a balanced view on the situation, trust him with control of the outcome. Ask his ideas for an equitable solution.

I think he is just frustrated, maybe at the weeds or maybe at something else in his life. He just wants to blame someone for it. Maybe he left the lid off the chemical and it rained and diluted the solution. Maybe it was old or never worked in the first place and he's embarrassed to admit it.

Anyway, lay it out to him and ask him what he thinks is truly fair to both parties. My bet is that you will be able to salvage this business relationship. If not, live and learn from it and never repeat it again. Don't let customers get that far behind in their payment to you."

Listening to your lawn care customers can make a big difference.

I know it sounds so cliche to say listen to your lawn care customers, but I think this is one of those simple issues that is way to often overlooked. One lawn care business got on the Gopher Lawn Care Business Forum and shared with us a story on how he has been able to grow his business by listening to his customers. What he found was, the more he listened, the happier the customer was with him and the more referrals he got from them!

He wrote "A few years back, I was getting ready to retire from the the Army after 25 years of service and decided I needed something else to keep me busy. So I decided to start a home maintenance and repair company in my spare time. Three years later, it is now doing really well for me. I deal with a lot of property managers and Realtors. As I explored more, I found there was a need for curb appeal in the housing market. So after some thought, I started a lawn care division and was blown away by the response from home owners needing service for their lawn care.

To date I have landed enough weekly, bi-monthly, and monthly accounts to keep me busy. I am now considering the possibility of offering snow removal this winter too.

One of the things I have done to promote my business was to partner up with a national painting company in town. Not only does this other business help me spread the word about my company but I am able to return the favor and spread the word about their company too. This other business owner has several property managers he works with that are always looking for people to maintain their property during vacant times.

A second activity I took part in was I became a member of a networking group in town. We meet every two weeks and there are always new faces there. The potential to expand my business's exposure is great! From this group I got a tip to sign up with a leads generating company that provides me with daily leads to new customers. So far this has the been the biggest bang for my advertising buck.

Thirdly, I use a lot of free internet advertising networks. I am on two different local community forums as well as post daily on a free regional classified ads site. They are both free. The internet can also be a great way to pro-actively look for potential commercial clients. When you find them in your area, save their contact information to a database and reach out to them with future mailings and phone calls. In the slow winter months I use direct mailing.

For people who have never run their own business before, my biggest piece of advice is don't easily give up. In the long run, perseverance will win out. Spend as much time as you can on marketing, marketing, marketing. I still handle all my marketing. It is the only way to keep your marketing cost down, which is important your first few years.

Another piece of helpful information for everybody starting a business is this. Listen to your customers. I was at a customer's house mowing her lawn and she happened to be home, so I took a few minutes to talk to her. I asked how she liked our service and if there was anything we could do to improve. She replied that she was very happy and we exceeded her expectations. Sometimes you have to read between the lines to hear what your customers want. During our initial conversation, all she said was she was allergic to chemicals. With that information in mind, I made the effort to find organic fertilizers. In our next conversation, I told her I had found an organic fertilizer that I would be applying to her lawn in the spring.

She was thrilled that I had paid attention and that I was looking out for her health. She also thanked me for edging her drive way because her previous lawn guys did not perform that service. Over time, due to the lack of edging, the dirt and grass had grown on to the concrete and it detracted from the home's curb appeal. So I remedied that situation and she was very happy about it.

I will also do other extra things that are not in the the original bid. If I am ahead of schedule, and do can things which take about 5 minutes worth of extra work. Things like cleaning up the street gutter in front of the driveway, picking up limbs in non-maintenance areas etc. Those extra 5 minutes during my weekly mowing shows my customers I am concerned about the looks of their property.

So remember to listen to what your customers have to say and that will lead to more job opportunities. I already landed two more jobs from this client and she has told me she is giving my name to a few friends who also are in need of my services."

Know your lawn care customer's quirks.

There is or should be a getting to know your customer period when you first get them signed up. Asking them questions and learning their quirks can lead to a long and profitable customer experience. Some lawn care business owners will try to force their view onto their customer and it tends to lead to conflict. Other lawn care business owners will learn their customer's quirks and focus on what makes them happy. Which path you choose to take will effect your business and your mental well being. Let's take a look at how two lawn care business owners handled two quirky customers and how these situations led two different outcomes.

A lawn care business owner wrote us on the Gopher Lawn Care Business Forum and shared a difficult situation he found himself in with a customer. He wrote "Ok so this lady has been a thorn in my side for the last 2 months. I should have seen it coming but I did not. Here's the situation.

I work a full time job and try to do all my mowing on Friday. So about 2 months ago on Friday morning about 9am I get a call from this lady that she would like an estimate for lawn care. I told her I could come by around noon and give her a quote. That won't do she says and wants me to come by at 3pm. I say ok.

So 3pm, 91 degrees, been up for 24 hours, humid as all h e l l. She agrees to the estimate and wants me to cut it right then. I am money hungry so I go for it. As I am finishing up she comes out and wants me to hit the weeds in her flower beds with the trimmer, ok fine. So the next week goes by without incident.

Then on week number 3 she comes out and follows me around and starts pointing out all the weeds in the flower bed that I did not 'trim.' As I finish the lawn this week I think to myself, next week I'm gonna talk to her about this trimming the weeds crap.

So the next week she calls me at 11am and wants to know if I am coming out 'because my grass is really high and it needs to be cut.' I told her that I had one more lawn before her and an estimate to give and I would be there around 12:30pm. So I get there and her power is out due to the previous nights storm and her sister died this week and the wake is at her house tonight and all these people are coming over and... yea OK just trim the weeds and get the heck out of there. The weed talk can wait a week.

So the next week is the 4th of July and I told her before I left that I was going to try to mow on Thursday because I was going out of town for the holiday. It poured down rained on Thursday. I called her and told her I would come over on Monday. So Monday at 10:15am she called (sounded really nasty) I need my lawn mowed and if you don't want to do it just let me know and I'll find someone else.

I'm thinking what the ??? So I get to her house around noon and she's not there. I mow and trim (even the darn weeds) and leave. I'll get paid next week.

So on Tuesday, she calls and leaves a message, I don't need you to mow my lawn anymore. When I called her back she said it was because she had to keep calling me to mow the lawn. Now bare in mind that all her calls were before noon on the day she was scheduled to have the lawn mowed. I was baffled. So I went to pick up the final payment. We have a contract that stipulates a 7 day notice in writing to cancel service. I mentioned this to her and she went ballistic. I cashed her check as soon as I left her house and I did not go back a week later."

Another lawn care business owner shared "you are going to run into these types of customers. What I have found is that if you can afford to get rid of them, do so. I usually include basic lawn care which is mow, edge, trim, and blow off grass in my monthly and annual agreements. I have a few customers who demand trimming and pruning be rolled into one monthly rate rather than billed separately as needed.

So in each case where I am asked to do extra trimming throughout the year, I estimate the length of time it will take to trim everything on the property and multiply that by my hourly rate, multiplied by 4 services a year then divided it by 12 months. I then add this figure to my monthly lawn rate. Still with me here? So where customers have me trim and clean up 2-3 times a year, I figured I do it more often (4 times annually) and keep it looking good.

I have one customer who seems to give a damn less about the lawn and is neurotic about the trimming and pruning? All summer last year every 2 weeks he was like 'aren't you gonna trim these damn hedges again?!' I would reply, 'No sir I did it 2 weeks ago.' He would then counter 'well I'm paying you to have them maintained all year long….! There's a few sprouts sticking out there! blah blah…..' 'Yes sir I'll knock those off for you….'

In the winter he kept saying stop running that hot mower (whatever the hell that means) over the lawn it doesn't need it! The grass is dormant then, but the weeds get a foot tall over a 2 week period. Then he says 'do some trimming while your here instead!' Last week I got a similar speech 'the rain makes the ground too soft to mow….. do some trimming instead!'

It's more like the guy wants 30 some odd trimming visits a year and 4 mowing visits instead of the other way around. We hit the end of our contract last month. He called me and where I should have just dropped him, we agreed to just trim more and mow less. We stayed at the same rate and continued another year. While the whole situation aggravated me all year long, the guy does like my work and even sent me a tip around Christmas. We just had a difference in expectations. In the end the customer is your boss (so to speak) so what the hell….. we'll try it his way! Hopefully this year will be better with him."

Help! I am having a communication breakdown with my customer.

When you have a communication breakdown with a customer, things can disintegrate fast. What was once a good interaction can quickly transform into being a terrible one. After you have been through a few of these situations, you start getting a feel for when situations are starting to take a turn for the worse. When you do and if you can catch them in time, you have a good chance at saving that customer. If you don't catch it in time, you may find yourself in a situation like this, wondering what to do.

A business owner wrote us on the Gopher Lawn Care Business Forum to get advice on how to deal with a customer relationship that soured. He wrote "in my lawn care contracts it says customer can exit the contract with a 30 day notice, however I have one customer who still hasn't paid my Feb payment and now it is March. This will make 2 months they will owe me for. They have been with me for 10 months until today when I saw another crew on their yard picking up trash and what not.

That lawn care company must have under cut my price because I had to beat a $90 a month plan to get them to sign in the first place! I don't know how to handle this. I am really mad. Should I take and spend the $80 court fees and see if I can get the $165 they owe me and sit there in court for 8 hours? Or should I just forget it?"

A second lawn care business owner said "send them a certified letter stating you owe me $X and have 1 week to pay from the receipt of the letter or you will be filing with the local court for petty claims on XX/XX/XX and note that they will owe you the cost for court as well as what they owe you plus a 10% late charge or whatever your late charge is. 9 out of 10 times they will pay.

Now if you did not have them sign a contract prior to doing any service for them, then I'd cut your losses and move on. Otherwise it's their word against yours. I don't care if it's a commercial or residential customer. To me, they are a client regardless of who they are. You need to get it all in writing. In your general service agreement make sure to put a late charge.

Mine says this.

'Payments not received within a five (5) day period after completion of service are subject to a late fee of $10.00 and will interrupt recurring services.'

In such a situation, the customer would owe me $80.00 + $10.00(late fee) + $20(court filing fee) = $110."

A third lawn care business owner shared "the first thing I would do is call them and ask if there is a problem with the invoice. Is their a problem with the service? Remind them you haven't been paid and when you dropped by there was another company performing services on their yard. Remind them you have a 30 day notice in your agreement.

Based on the feedback it will tell you what to do. You can file a mechanics lien against their property, which would get you paid at the time the property was sold. I am not sure what it costs there to do this but for $80.00, it would not be worth my time."

A forth business owner said "It just sounds like a communication break down.

   * First did they sign anything?
   * Second, were they unhappy with their contract? You were mowing for them for 10 months. I am surprised they didn't say

anything to you. Were they unhappy with the mowing?

Did they give any notice that they were moving to another company?

I guess I am always surprised when I hear stories like this because I try to keep in good contact and connection with the home owners. I try to make sure that they are happy with their services and that there isn't anything unspoken. It is when things are unspoken that it becomes uneasy like with what you are dealing with now."

Keep these thoughts in mind when dealing with your customers. The less you communicate with them, the more chances will arise for conflict to exist. Address any issues early before they become problems. Don't let customers go two months without paying you, without asking what is going on. Find the problem, find a solution, and move forwards.

ESTIMATING

Pricing lawn care and yard cleanups.

How to price lawn mowing or a yard cleanup seems to be one of the more popular questions asked on the Gopher Lawn Care Business Forum. Many new lawn care business owners tend to be lost with this and understandably so, it can be very difficult to wrap your mind around proper bidding concepts.

To help shed more light on this topic, a lawn care business owner shared with us how he comes up with the prices he charges. As you will see here, there is a method to it and it is scientific. If you find yourself on a job site guessing what you should charge, you need to rethink your bidding procedures.

He wrote "I hear a lot of talk about HOW to bid this and HOW to bid that or is this a good price to charge for this, is this too much or too little?

I know that every job is different, but the pricing methods shouldn't change, providing you have set up a standards price list for service you'll be providing when you began your business venture. This list should have been one of the first things done before even bidding to the first customer. Without a price list, how will you know what amount to charge for each service you provide?

When choosing the services you are going to provide, you should have a price to go along with that service. Now there are different charges for added difficulty, say you charge $45 min for cutting up to 3000 sq ft of level to slightly rolling lawn. Add $10.00 to that for every extra 1,000 sq. ft and $5 for every step UP of difficulty. (excessive trees, extended plant areas, hilly or steep ditches that require more trimming time).

Let's say you have been cutting and performing some small

landscaping details all summer and you have a customer ask for a fall clean up. You should have a good idea of how long it will take to clean up the leafs.

If not here is a common rule; For every 1,000 sq.ft. of yard it should take 1 man, 1.5 hrs. @ your hourly rate, if he/she is to blow into wind row and remove. (NOTE: to some who didn't or don't know, using wind rows make collecting leaves faster and easier to manage and pick up). To clarify, a wind row is when you blow all grass clipping or leafs into a long narrow row, instead of one or to big piles, this makes it easier to clean up and is faster all around.

Clean up around plant areas for every 500 sq. ft. should take 1 man 1.5 hrs. to hand rake and blow into yard. Also you would want to add gutter clean out in this automatically at a rate of $1.00 per linear foot, now you will have dumping charges for this, if you don't have a place to dump for free, this charge should be 1.85 times the cost of dumping at your local dump and this will cover expenses (dump charges, fuel & time). ex. dump charge cost $85.00 x 1.85 = $157.25. Now let's put this all together with a yard clean up example and see what comes of it.

4,000 sq ft of yard = 6 man hrs @ $45 per hr.= $270.00
1,000 sq ft of plant area = 3 man hrs @ $45 per hr = $135.00
60 linear feet of gutter = $1.00 per Ln ft. x 60 Ln ft. = $60.00
Dump/Removal Charge = $85 @ 1.85 multiplier = $157.25

Total charges for the clean up $622.25 not bad for a days work. If you have an extra hand you should be able to complete this in 4 hours. Pay you helper $8 - $10 per hour if you have more jobs for that day or just pay them $100 bucks for that job.

Let's look at the profit and loss statement for this job;
EXPENSE;
- Fuel cost for truck and blowers $30

- Dumping charge $85
- Extra labor $100
- Total expense $215.00

P&L = $407.25 you just made $100.00 per hour by using a helper. The P&L will go up only slightly if you do this on your own.

The point I'm trying to make is set your prices and stick to them. Every job is different but the hourly charges per man hour and flat rates should stay the same for every customer. If you charge one customer one thing and then charge another a different amount for the same job this will put doubt in their mind.

ex. Customer calls wants the patio pressure washed the patio is of normal dirtiness and it is 10ft × 15ft = 150 sq ft. You charge this customer $1.00 per sq ft. equaling $150.00. They tell a neighbor and their deck is of equal dirtiness and it is 8ft × 20ft = 160 sq ft you charge them $1.50 per sq ft. equaling $240.00. This customer is not going to be happy and probably won't call you back nor will the first customer because you have put doubt into their minds and made them wonder is this guy for real is he just throwing #'s out there or what.

Don't ever leave room for doubt or a question of your integrity as a business owner/operator. YOU WILL lose if you do."

Know how to price lawn mowing jobs.

There can never be enough discussions on pricing lawn care jobs. At first when you get started, you may eyeball a property and come up with a figure based on a guess, but there are much better ways to do this. As your business is around longer, you will get an idea of what your operating costs are. Knowing these costs is crucial to making a profit. If you know them, you will be able to tell which of the jobs you are making money on, which you are breaking even on and which you are losing money on.

Just because you are out there working all day long doesn't mean you are making money! You could actually be paying your customers to work on their property and not even know it. Have you ever thought about that? When you lose money on a job, that is exactly what you are doing. Paying to do the work. Doesn't that sound crazy? But it happens everyday.

A member of the Gopher Lawn Care Business Forum shared with us some insight he has learned over the years being in the business. He wrote "from the experience I have with many new lawn care business owners, I have found that knowing how to estimate your lawn mowing jobs is a huge issue.

I think the very first issue you have to confront is cost of doing business.

Can you imagine a successful manufacturing plant manager shrugging his shoulders when asked what his actual marginal cost is for each additional unit?

Before I got into the lawn care business, I was an accountant with a manufacturing company. We knew exactly how much each part cost, that was required for each and every product we made. We even practically knew how much electricity was needed to make each product! Nothing was overlooked.

To be successful over the long haul, you need to adopt a very structured approach to bidding jobs. Let me pose a question for you to think about. How many guys do you think bid a $40 grass cutting job simply because their friends said that's how much to charge?

I think most everyone of us did that when we first started. We had little idea of costs and little idea of what the market would actually bear.

Here's an example of what happens though. The going rate of residential lawns is $40 per cut in a certain area of the country. But, someone gets a late start or is in need of new customers. So, that guy drops his price and starts bidding at $30. Then someone else hears how this guy is doing 10 yards per day and brings home $300 per day. This third guy decides he can do a couple yards each day after work or school. So, he loads up a barely functioning push lawn mower into his truck and starts doing lawns for $20 or $25 for extra money.

Over the course of a year or two, lowballing drops the price out of the market and no one makes money. The guy charging $20 gives up and just continues with his day job. The guy charging $30 has an equipment breakdown that he can't afford to fix and has to drop out. The only one left to pick up the pieces is the professional who has a steady structure of well paying customers. Prices begin to rise and the whole cycle starts over again. I wonder about the length of the cycle. 5 years?

Here is another example. Say you charge $1/sq.ft. for pressure washing. If the going rate is $1, that is only one half of the equation. A company still has to know it's costs. If a company has a brand new high pressure washer, say a high flow warm water pressure washer in addition to a 250 gallon tank carrying filtered water in an enclosed dual axle trailer and a brand new $45 grand F-350 to haul it all, doing deck work might not be the best use of his resources. His costs alone might approach $1 to $2 per sq ft. Somewhere there is an equilibrium point. Instead of doing deck work, his equipment might be better suited for industrial cleaning and paint stripping.

That's why nobody can really ever tell anyone else exactly how much they should bid on a job. One guy might be able to make a great living at $1/sq ft. while another guy might go broke.

All this illustrates the need for a business plan long before you get heavy into the business. You have to know what the going rate per hour is and what your costs per hour are. You have to know what types of customers to target and what equipment you will need to service those customers once you get them.

I don't think a business plan solves all questions by any means. But, it gives a good basis to begin with and it can always be adjusted later."

How to charge for year round lawn care.

There are many situations you will run into as a lawn care business owner where you may wonder if you should be charging extra for certain services. A member of the Gopher Lawn Care Business Forum had an interesting question along these lines when he asked "if you are providing lawn care for a customer and a storm occurs that causes sticks and leaves to fall on the lawn, you obviously can't cut the lawn with out moving the debris first. How do you go about charging extra for yard clean up? Or do you even charge them?

I guess I am stuck on at what point do you start charging extra for picking up and blowing leaves."

One lawn care business owner shared "here is what I do. When I give a bid for yard service, I try to figure these things in to my bid from the beginning. I will look at the property and evaluate how many trees there are, what kinds of trees, etc. For example Willows are especially messy to work with. When I calculate my service charge it includes the cleanup costs year round. So my price might seem a little high through the summer months, but it evens out through the messy winter months. I try not to charge for cutting only, I try to charge for maintaining the entire yard."

Another lawn care business owner had an opposing view. "I've found from my bidding experience, for it to be different. If I include everything from trimming, pruning, weeding & clean ups all in one price, I miss a lot of bids. But those customers who go with it also want their entire property to look picture perfect all year round and tend to nag you to death about every little thing. When this happens, there can be times where I only get half my mowing list done for the day. If this repeats everyday, I just can't catch up.

My normal lawn care service consists of mow, edge, trim, and blow off. All extras are separately requested/suggested, sold, invoiced, and scheduled.

People understand that extra work above and beyond our agreement means an additional charge.

But when someone wants say trimming included in a monthly service bill, I look and say ok this will cost $150 to trim say 4 times a year. If I add $600 to the total for the year and divide by 12 it becomes an extra $50 a month fee. From my experience, the customers simply won't pay it. Instead, they want to haggle it down and add $20-30 a month and then if I agree they drive me nuts all year with 'trim this up again ok? Aren't you gonna hit those bushes again, it's been 3 weeks…' It drives me nuts!

But if I keep the services separate, most customers will let it go until the landscaping is getting a little overgrown. So I maybe only get to trim it 3 times a year but I will charge more since it's overgrown.

When I handle my billing like this, the customer is happy and I get all the 'WOW, It looks much better, thank you so much' type of gratitude. They get their landscape maintained when they deem it's ready to be maintained (and don't expect anything in between), and I still get paid for trimming a years worth of landscape growth.

Which way is ultimately better is up for individual decision, but my vote is to separate the services and bill for them."

How to raise your lawn care prices and not lose customers.

It usually takes about one full lawn care season to get you to a point where you begin to understand your overhead and operational costs effect your profit. At the end of your first season, you may look at your bank account and realize with all your efforts, you have very little money to show for it. If you find this to be the case, you may want to consider either cutting costs or raising your prices. But if you raise your lawn mowing prices, won't you lose your customers? Not if you do it properly. Let's look at a question that was posted on the Gopher Lawn Care Business Forum on how to do this.

A lawn care business owner wrote "after my first year in business, it is clear to me that I will need to raise some of my customer's prices. This was my first year. I inherited some of my customers, whose properties I had maintained for several seasons, from a previous company I worked for. After analyzing my costs and income, wouldn't you know it, these 'inherited customers' are primarily the customers who are under priced! The previous business owner low balled a lot of his clients and many of them have had the same price for a number of years. It's no wonder he went out of business.

However, I don't know how to go about raising their prices and am afraid of losing some of my customers by doing so. Does anybody have advice on how to present this? I want to bring this news to the customer in a gentle, non-offensive manner… explaining the economy, rising costs etc etc etc. Please help."

One lawn care business owner suggested "I personally would not send my customers a letter no matter how many you may have. It's like breaking up with your girlfriend over a text message. It's kind of cheap to me. I would go around and speak with all of my clients personally and just have a chat with them. My clients like me for being like that. Most businesses just send a letter in the mail. I go right up to their front door and talk with them personally. To me that is more respectful as a business owner.

How much are you thinking on raising the prices? You should figure that out first. How you word it is up to you. If you know your customers personally, it will obviously be easier to confront them about this. If you don't, your main goal is to 'complete' things in a polite fashionable manner. Even if they get pissed and you lose them. Keep a professional attitude, apologize and offer them a business card and a free service so they have time to find another company to suit their needs. You have to be upfront....not strict ....but upfront ... and polite.

Something I have found and you may too, is my cheaper customers complain the most. It is amazing how much they can complain. Early on, I had a guy that I only charged $25 for a full leaf removal service. He had a 2 acre yard! I did this because he was a friend of the family. So I gave him a dirt cheap price. Every time he would come out of his house, he would pick these odd places that he wanted leafs removed from. One day, he came up to me and said that I was not doing a good enough job. The leaves were still falling as I was cleaning them up! I told him that I got everything cleaned up but since the leaves were still falling, they were covering his yard back up again.

He wanted me to keep cleaning them up until they were done falling. I had finally had it and said "ok.... give me $150 a week until leafs stop falling and I can do that for you." He threw a fit and I got so pissed I terminated the service after I was done with the job. I was definitely glad to get rid of him. But if I had handled it better, I probably wouldn't have been in that situation to begin with."

A second shared "I think you are doing yourself a disservice by not raising the prices to the current going rate or at least close to it.

If you admit a lawn's price should be raised by a certain dollar figure and you only raise it by half that, you are leaving money on the table per mow. At say 40 cuts per year that can really add up per customer over the course of a year.

It can be a big chunk but customers are aware that prices rise occasionally and your customers probably will not balk at a reasonable amount. They still won't like it but if you give quality service they will likely agree. Quality service is the key here. If they have no complaints with your work and dependability, a rise in prices alone will not make them drop you.

When it comes to raising prices, I've always found personalized letters with personal follow-ups a few days later work great. I know you may get different opinions on this matter but I think it comes down to your personality and how close you are with your customers. If you can talk to them, that is great, if you would rather send a letter, then go that route. I would just suggest not trying to raise everyone's price at once. Do it in test groups and see how it goes first on a smaller scale."

How to estimate a top soil installation job.

Have you been asked by any of your lawn care customers to give them a bid on adding some topsoil to their property? Did you find you were at a loss as to how to estimate such a job? A lawn care business owner had this issue and asked on the Gopher Lawn Care Business Forum "I need help on an estimate for a top soil job. The area is 40ft x 50ft. Screened top soil in my area will cost me $20.00 a ton. What should I charge to perform this job?"

One lawn care business owner suggested "around here a cubic yard of top soil is about $25 wholesale. It runs about $50 bucks a cu.yd. to deliver it within 9 miles if I don't pick it up myself. I recently bid on a property that came to 1,806 sq feet. I figured I would need 13 cubic yards or about 5.5 tons of topsoil. The cost for the topsoil came to about $425 after delivery.

This job required me to remove the old sod, haul it away, pay for disposal etc etc. To bid this, I doubled the costs of the materials to $850 then I needed to add 20 man hours at $65 an hour. Keep in mind this is some back breaking work, to remove sod then spread the top soil. I figured $300 to remove the sod from the site and dispose of it. It came to a total of $2,400 for the bid."

Another lawn care business owner said "as a topsoil supplier, I found most customers want to do the job themselves. They just need materials. Larger jobs requiring a tractor rather than shovel and rake are bid between $65-$125 hour plus soil. I always bid or estimate jobs, portal to portal. This means include the total cost of your time to get there and back to your place of business as well as materials used.

Almost without exception if I deliver topsoil or mulch on a street and dump it in the front yard, shortly after wards I will get calls from neighbors for more work. I leave at least two business cards with every invoice, so the customer can hand them to neighbors. Short loads of 1 to 3 yards are always delivered in a pick-up style dump. During the planting season I am constantly on the road delivering top soil.

Quite a few times I have seen lawn care business owners simply don't know how to calculate the cubic yards required for the job. The simple formula is:
square feet x inches of thickness needed x .0033 = cubic yards

Using the example of a job requiring 40′ X 50′ of top soil, that is 2,000 sq.ft.

If I assume a 2″ topdressing depth, I get the following equation: 2,000 X 2 X 0.0033= 13.2 cubic yards.

The formula gets really simple for 1″ depth. Just multiply the square footage by 0.0033. In his case it would look like this: 2000 X 0.0033= 6.6 yards

If you're in the business of topsoil & mulch you can create a cheat sheet based on depth. Then you can just plug in the square footage. This is handy for your secretary to use when a customer calls and doesn't know how much they need.

1″: SF X .0033
2″: SF X .0066
3″: SF X .0099
4″: SF X .0132
….and so on…."

Passing on a large lawn care bid.

Most lawn care business owners tend to think you need to take every bid that comes your way. The truth of it though is sometimes you need to know when to say no. Sometimes scaling up to take on a larger bid can throw off the delicate balance you have created in your business. More employees, more trucks, more mowers. All of these things that will be needed for larger commercial lawn care jobs need to be managed. A business owner only has so much time in a day and can't manage everything. So some elect to stay at a certain size they are comfortable with. Have you reached that point? Or are you still looking to grow? Let's look at how one lawn care business owner handled this situation he discussed on the Gopher Lawn Care Business Forum.

He wrote "I had a few messages on my phone today that I listened to on the way home after a long day. One shocked me, it was the school board from my town wanting a quote on lawn care. I was thinking this was strange as it should have to go for tender but the man sounded pretty agitated with the current provider. I know this lawn care company well as I have taken a few of their accounts. As much as it hurts, I am going to have to pass on this job though. I know the company that does this job uses 4 trucks, three wide area mowers, and a pile of ZTR and push mowers. Adding another 16 employees to perform this job doesn't interest me. My company is already putting me in a situation where I have become an office manager, which I don't like and won't do. I have been thinking for a while now that I may need to downsize.

Money is not the issue in this case nor is getting equipment. Prepayment is not an option with government contracts. The problem is that it's a massive account. I currently have a staff of 17 and do not want to even be this large, you wouldn't believe the amount paper work that is involved!"

I am sure many lawn care business owners will wrestle with this issue as they grow. Do you think there is any rule of thumb as to when to go with a job and when to pass?

I am sure there is money in this job that would certainly make most jump all over it, but there seems to be a downside to having to scale up so quickly.

How can you hold yourself back when presented with something that might be outside your businesses comfort zone?

"Yes there is money in the job. The school district is willing to sign a five year contract, subject to a performance clause in the contract which is fine by me.

We are already as big or bigger than I want to be. I am flattered they called me and we spoke twice today. They seem pretty intent on my taking over but I am honestly not interested. It might be next year but I have to find someone to manage the business as I would rather be out working. I hate being in the office. This isn't why I started my business.

I handle a situation like this by being very straight forward. This year I have 159 landscaping projects, 196 lawn spraying clients and close to 90 lawn mowing jobs. I simply do not want to expand any further at this time."

Do you think it ever hurts customer relations when you turn work down and possibly say you are just too swamped right now and you can't take on anything more?

Is there a bad way this could be handled and should be avoided?

"Yes and no. Many understand and they really appreciate your honesty. Some don't understand and wonder why you just don't expand further.

This business was supposed to be a fun retirement hobby business for me. I wanted to work with my family and perhaps employ a few friends, however, the company took on a life of it's own and it's been desperately difficult for me to manage. I receive 4 to 11 inquiries a day, every day that in itself is a full time job.

I think the worst way to handle this is to take on the work without having the ability to do it. I have been in business long enough to know when to put the brakes on or something will blow up."

How to bid one customer with multiple properties.

At some point while you are operating your lawn care business, you are going to come across a customer who owns multiple properties and will want you to bid on all of them at once. These properties might be residential or they may be commercial. How should you present your bid to such a customer and look professional doing it even when you may be unsure how they want the bid presented? That is a question asked on the Gopher Lawn Care Business Forum.

A lawn care business owner shared with us his situation when he wrote "I am a fairly new business owner. This is my third year in business. I have a web site but do not advertise any where else. I have gotten plenty of business all through word of mouth. The secret to it is if you just go the extra mile with each and every customer, before you know it, people will just come out of the wood work looking for your business and pay very well for your services.

Recently I had a property manager call and ask if I would submit bids for all of their accounts. This totals 38 accounts in all! I did not want to look unprofessional or anything, so I didn't ask how he wanted the bid presented. But now I am wondering how the bids should look. Should I list all the accounts on one page with a break down of service fees with a weekly and monthly price quote? Or should I have each bid separate from all others on separate paper?"

One lawn care business owner suggested "first off, you shouldn't ever worry about asking the customer how they want the bids presented. This won't make you look like an amateur. The fact that they didn't tell you how they wanted it most likely means they have no idea themselves which way would work best. You always should ask the customer what they want and give it to them.

With the situation you are in now, you could print it out both ways so you are prepared either way the property manager wants it presented.

Usually the property manager will present you with a cover letter to the bid package detailing how to submit. However, if one is not available, as I said, it doesn't hurt to ask. In my experience you should provide a separate quote for each property. These properties may be held under different board of directors / owners and the property management company will have to present them to each."

I underbid a job, what can I do about it now?

Have you ever found yourself in a situation where you underbid a job and within a short time of starting it, you realized you were going to have to eat some serious costs to complete it? If you have, you are not alone. This kind of thing happens from time to time, especially when you are new to the business or you are offering a new service you haven't quite yet gotten under your belt. When you do find yourself in such a situation, the first thing to remember is don't make it any worse than it is. Follow these simple tips and you may be able to turn a money losing job into a profitable one.

A member of the Gopher Lawn Care Business Forum wrote "I've been stuck on this one job for almost a month. Tomorrow I will hopefully be finally finished. When I initially wrote up the contract for this job, I had put the date range at only 5 days. It's almost been 30 and I've been eating the cost on this job each and every day since. I might as well have written the contract and billed myself.

This past month I've been struggling. All profits from the other jobs I'm currently busting my butt on, have been used to pay the expenses for this disaster job I'm on. Basically I don't feel as if I should be paying for these people's yard service. They know they screwed me, as they can see this project wound up being a lot bigger that was initially bid on.

If I were smart I would have just pulled away when my costs exceeded what I bid the job to be in total. I guess just because of my kindness and hard work ethic, I didn't want to just say screw you and stop the job. Instead I'm finishing it because I don't know what else to do."

One lawn care business shared "when you find yourself in this situation, there is nothing wrong with going back to a customer and working out a solution both parties can agree to. In my experience most, not all, but most will understand that we all have bills to pay and sometimes our estimates are not on the mark. There have been time where I eat the costs, however those are rare. The few times this has happened to me, I usually have a heart to heart with the customer and have found they respect this and generally speaking we always walk away happy.

The thing is, you don't want to wait too long to have this talk. That is a pitfall many new business owners tend to fall into. In fact, the sooner you realize there is a problem, the better it is to bring it to the customer's attention. Show them how an unforeseen circumstance is going to cause you to spend more time or money to complete the job. Work out the problem before you continue and keep everyone happy."

Trailer park lawn care bid.

Performing lawn care for a trailer park can differ a little from mowing residential properties. The plots are usually a lot smaller but there is also a lot more trimming than mowing needed. What's the best way to price a mobile home bid? Is it even worth it? That is what one member of the Gopher Lawn Care Business Forum was wondering when he asked us about such a bid.

He wrote "There is a mobile home park in my area that is up for bidding. It has approximately 70 to 80 mobile homes that are spaced 20-30 feet apart.

   * Trimming 125-140 ft per mobile home
   * I have a 42in deck mower (will be expanding if I get the job)
   * Edging none
   * There are about 40 trees to cut and trim around the property

They want to find out from me, how much I would charge per mobile home. I was thinking about $15 to $20. Is that to low, too high or just about right? What would you charge per mobile home?"

One lawn care business owner shared "I currently mow a mobile home park with 14 trailer and about 107k sq ft. It takes me 4 hours to trim and mow. I charge $20 per trailer."

A second business owner said "that could easily take 2 full days to complete with all that trimming. So if you figure it takes, oh let's say 20 hrs to complete and if you base it on $60/hr, that would be $1,200.00. That would be my lowest price doing it solo."

A third lawn care business owner said "I currently mow 15 mobile homes in a park I live in at. I charge $20 for each one.

None of them take me more then 15 minutes to do by myself. I did it at that price to get more customers and referrals and it has worked for me. I still make a profit off of each one but it is a very small profit. However, the referrals I get from the job make it worth while."

A final view on it was "$15 to $20 seems reasonable. If the trailer park owner wants to know how much for each, go and make a list of the ones that are smaller and have less trimming. Price those at $15 and the bigger ones or with more trimming, price at $20. It's hard to imagine them taking more than about 20 minutes to mow.

You are looking at $1,050 - $1,600 for the job.

Approximately 18 to 28 hours worth of work… 2 to 3 days depending on how fast and how long you work."

EQUIPMENT

A great way to find low cost lawn care equipment.

Are you just getting your lawn care business started and looking for ways to get some lawn care equipment to get you started? If you want to find some great stuff that is cheap and nearby, consider doing what this lawn care business owner did. He shared a great tip on how to do this on the Gopher Lawn Care Business Forum.

He wrote "I just got my lawn care business started last month and I already own all of the starting equipment I need. This is something you might want to try. I purchased much of my power equipment from sales by people who were foreclosed on. They are easy to find and the prices are fantastic. I bought a 2007 lawn tractor with a 46" deck for $300.00. A leaf blower for $35.00. An open 5' x 10' trailer and other equipment for $250.00. I found all of this at one sale! At another, I picked up a core aerator and a commercial spreader for $100.00."

That sounds like a great way to get started on the cheap! But how do you go about finding where these sales will be?

"Home foreclosures are reported in our local paper. I write down the addresses when I find them and then check for moving, yard and garage sales with the same address. Obviously, the people are going to be moving to an apartment and have the choice of selling or storing. But it seems most just want to sell.

Most of these people are in over their head and have let the lawn go because they have negative equity in the property. So you will want to market to these homes as soon as they are sold."

Stander vs sitting? Which mower is best for you?

When you are looking to buy a new lawn mower and thinking about getting something besides a walk behind, you have a bunch of options you can choose from. Some mowers allow you to stand on a platform while others let you sit down. Which one is better for you? You may think sitting down is better but you might be surprised to find that is not what lawn care business owners are saying.

A lawn care business owner wrote us on the Gopher Lawn Care Business Forum and asked "I have been a fan of ZTR mowers for a while now but I'm open to some advice on what I should be looking for in a new mower. I am considering a stand-on mower next. The more I look around the more I see other lawn care business owners using stand-ons. These machines look slick and compact, but I'd like more information, or reviews about them. What are the pros and cons on having such a machine?

One of the benefits I can see immediately is their compact size. I could fit 3 stand-on mowers on my trailer."

Another lawn care business owner said "I love my stand on mower. I will never purchase another zero turn tractor again, unless I land a property with a lot of acres. But even then I would buy a tractor, not a lawn mower.

The standers have great viewing all around the mower. They have a quick response, easier to work on and maintain, and awesome to operate on slopes.

The only down side I can think of is that they can be a little light on the rear tires when turning. It takes a little while to get used to just like any new mower though."

A second member shared "I like standing on the spring loaded platform. Your legs act like shock absorbers instead of your lower back which can take a pounding in the seated position all day. Don't get me wrong I do love my 62" ztr which I use on the more open larger acreage accounts but my stander is a lot more nimble and better to use on my average lawn accounts. I have some pretty bad re-occurring back problems, and my ztr will just slam my lower back constantly. I know it sounds weird but standing up on the spring loaded foot deck is great.

The longest I spend on my stander is about 3 hours non stop. By the end of mowing that account I am ready to get off. Even with that said I have found walk behinds are the most fatiguing type of mower made and I rarely use them."

When you are looking to purchase a new mower, consider the size of the properties you are servicing and whether you want your back or your legs to take the shock. If your lawns are average sized, you may find a stander is the best mower for you.

Lawn care equipment needed for startups.

When you start up your lawn care business, you can go a couple of ways when it comes to equipment. You can either take the low dough approach, which means the cheapest equipment you can find, or spend some big bucks to get new commercial equipment. Which way you go depends a lot on the amount of start up capital you have. If you are broke, obviously you need to start dirt cheap, but as we will see in this discussion from the Gopher Lawn Care Business Forum, cheap equipment won't cut it for long.

A new lawn care business owner wrote "I am just starting up my lawn & landscape company as we speak. I'm planning on getting a truck and enclosed trailer to start. What width and length of a trailer should I go with? I'm debating on 7'×16' or 8'×16'. Also, what equipment would you recommend to start out with? My area is 1/3 to 1/2 acre subdivisions."

One lawn care business owner suggested "being that you are new to this and aren't sure if you will do this for long, you should probably start out with the mower you use to mow your home lawn and a small 6' x 12' trailer or work out of a pickup. Instead of spending money on equipment now, put your money into marketing. Keep your eye out for used commercial grade equipment and trailer as you start to get more customers. There are a lot of really good deals online. My own biggest regret was spending money on two new mowers and a weed eater when I first got started. I simply didn't need all that equipment or those payments."

Another lawn care business owner had different advice, "I was in business for about two weeks with a residential tractor mower I had, when I decided to go big or go home. I spent about $7,500 on a brand new commercial ztr mower. It increased my productivity tremendously, increase the quality of my cut, and gave me peace of mind. I felt better knowing it was new and under warranty. I didn't want anyone else's old equipment headaches.

I don't regret that purchase at all. In fact I bought a 2nd machine less than a year later and plan to buy a 3rd in the spring. For me, to be a professional in this industry I gotta be running professional grade gear. Yeah you can buy used commercial gear but who knows what kind of hidden problems you might end up with? My machines have paid for themselves many times over, even before they past their warranty. Any extra time you are able to use them after the payments and warranty expire (without major overhaul type repairs) is all gravy for your business.

The same thing applies to trucks. Some people, and I used to be one of them, would buy older cheap trucks and run them until the wheels fell off. Granted there were no payments but the headaches were nonstop. The brakes need to be replaced, transmission issues, battery, alternators, front end problems. Then I realized, I wasn't paying a monthly truck payment but I was still making payments. $200 here, $80 there, $400 for transmission work, $100 for a muffler, $150 for a starter etc. I decided to bite the bullet and bought my 1st new truck a few years back. Yup the payments still sucked but the damn thing started every morning and got me to the job site on time. No headaches and no missed work while fixing it. I haven't owned a clunker since.

I felt I needed to dive in head first to make sure I would succeed. If you half ass it and don't invest much time, money, or energy then it's easy to walk away. If you are all in, you will make it work.

As far as trailers go, I needed to be able to secure my gear at night from theft and I wanted to have the trailer all lettered to look like a rolling billboard. I run a 6'×12' cargo craft enclosed trailer. It has served me pretty well thus far."

A lawn care equipment dealer's recommendations.

Everyone has their own view of what kind of lawn care equipment you should get when you are new to the lawn care industry. Some will want to buy cheap equipment, others will spend their entire savings buying the most expensive equipment they can get their hands on. But what would a lawn care equipment dealer recommend? Surely they have seen many new lawn care business owners make many mistakes when it comes to buying equipment. Here is a view from a member of the Gopher Lawn Care Business Forum who also owns an outdoor power equipment business.

He shared "I am obviously speaking from the other side of the fence, as an equipment dealer, but I have to say, if you are going to purchase equipment, purchase good quality equipment. Equipment does not have to be spray painted with a bold color and have a fancy name on it but it does have to be of good quality. Be sure the equipment you purchase is designed to do what you are planning to do with it. I have been servicing equipment for over 10 years and have seen the death of many cheap trimmers, mowers, and accessories due to one thing: they were being used for 'commercial use' when they were intended for consumer usage. There is a big difference in the design between these different categories.

When I say commercial use I mean that you are using it for more than just your own yard. For example, a light weight trimmer may be light and easier to use while being less fatiguing to operate, but what about the fact that they may not last all season? Or that it may die on you when you are half way done with a job? Do you want to have to leave a good customer's job half trimmed or half mowed just because you were too cheap to buy good equipment and it quit in the middle of Saturday afternoon? Granted, any equipment can quit at any given time, but good quality equipment is far less likely to do so.

Then there is the matter of what type of business are you running? If you are the neighborhood kid who is just getting his feet wet in the business or earning some summer money by push mowing a few neighborhood yards, then you may be able to get by with a simple, used push mower and a cheap $60-$70 trimmer. On the other hand, if you are trying to operate a credible business, with real customers, you need to realize the customer is the one who feeds you. You want to attract customers who are willing to pay you and refer you to their friends, family, and neighbors.

I know each person is in business for themselves and with a slightly different point of view but remember, whether you are mowing 50 residential yards or 50 commercial lawns, you need to appear professional to your customers. If your customer drives nice vehicles or has a nice lawn, they are probably going to expect a decent looking piece of equipment on their lawn and a decent looking lawn care truck parked in front of their house.

Each brand and type of outdoor power equipment has a different life span. Most consumer equipment is typically not intended to run more than one or two seasons while only mowing one lawn. Commercial equipment is intended to be used all day, every day, for season after season. Some consumer models may last longer than others but none are intended to hold up like the commercial equipment. Many commercial products can have a lifespan greater than 10 times a consumer model's lifespan.

Typically the deciding factor is in what kind of materials are used to manufacture the equipment. When you compare a cheap big box push mower with a commercial mower, you will find the commercial is heavier. It is made out of heavier and higher quality materials.

My personal favorite brand of 2-cycle equipment has almost their entire line of equipment as commercial grade. Then when you compare other manufacturers who have about 1/2 of their equipment as consumer grade you see the difference comes in the quality of materials.

While one manufacturer uses the best materials available in their cylinders: Chrome plated cylinder with 2-ring pistons. Most of their competitors use only one ring on the pistons. Commercial engines are built with tolerances so tight that you can remove the piston ring from a new engine and start the engine with no ring. This is impossible on most other brands. Commercial brands also use bigger bearings and thus there is less wear on the larger bearings.

I would not recommend someone go out and spend $20-$30 grand in equipment their first year. But then again, it is your business and only you know what your expectations are. I can't dream your dream nor can I live your dream. Just make wise, informed, and well thought out decisions. Buy equipment that was designed to be used the way you are intending to use it."

A mower hour meter tip that can save you thousands $$$.

Most commercial mowers will come with a factory installed hour meter on them. These meters are very important. They can tell you when you need to change your oil. When your mower will need an overhaul. Most importantly, they help determine the resale value of your mower. Whether you are buying a mower or selling one. The hour meter is very important. But what happens when you leave your mower to sit over a period of time and come back to find your mower meter has added thousands of extra hours? This is a situation a member of the Gopher Lawn Care Business Forum ran into. Here he discusses what problems occurred from it and how he resolved it.

He wrote, "today I went into my garage just to start up my mower. It's winter here and there is about a foot of snow on the ground. I figured I would just start it up. Well the engine didn't turn over. I was a little concerned so I got a space heater to warm up the garage. Later I went to start up the mower again and it wouldn't do anything.

I accidentally left the key in the 'on' position. The battery was dead. That really wasn't a problem. The real problem was the mower hour meter read like 2,173 hours!!

I had about 146 hours when I put it into storage. What can or should I do???? My new machine is reading like an 8 year old work horse???? What now??? Help!!!"

One lawn care business owner wrote "call your dealership and explain you left the key on and what happened and you want the hour meter reset. They should be able to do it for you. Otherwise the resale value of your mower will be next to nothing.

I have seen this happen on tractors so I know it can be done, but get it done. It is very, very important in your case. A few hours is one thing but 2,000 hours is going to really cost you come the time you sell it.

I suspect you have may have also burnt the points out of it by leaving the key on that long. "

A lawn mower dealer shared "first I will address the points and condenser issue and then I will tell you why you probably don't have to worry about that in this case.

To answer the question about the points, if your engine has points and the ignition was left on for any extended period of time (and the points were closed), the points are most likely burned up. When the points are closed, it creates a complete circuit that is in essence a dead short. If that is the case, not only are the points probably shot, but so is the rest of the ignition components.

The problem with leaving your ignition turned on is that the dead short will cause your points to burn up and can ruin the coil and possibly other ignition components and wiring. I have seen points welded together as a result of the key had been left on.

I would recommend you not try to fix this yourself. In this case the mower is too new and still under warranty. If you take anything apart, the warranty will most likely become void. A lot more than just the points could have gone bad. Take it to the dealer and have them service it and explain what happened so they can reset the hour meter.

Not all mowers will experience such issues as their hour meter is wired to the electric clutch. So the meter is running only when the blades are turning. The few hours when the engine is idling is not important. Such mower wiring will keep an accident like you described from happening.

But everyone should be aware this can be a problems and be careful not to do this."

BUSINESS

The lawn care business & learned helplessness.

Have you ever looked around and seen some people tend to excel at almost anything they do while others seem to fail? When you look at the businesses or projects you have been involved with, have you found more success or more failure and wondered why that happens? Are you lucky? Are you jinxed? If you happen to find that you don't perform as well as you'd like to in the business world or in life, you may want to research the mental condition of learned helplessness. A member of the Gopher Lawn Care Business Forum brought this topic up and it was a fascinating discussion.

He wrote "I had a great discussion with a close friend tonight. We discussed some of the aspects that cause people to fail at business (and life). When you have a quiet 30 minutes, sit down and do some research on the topic of 'Learned Helplessness.' It's a condition that effects some people where they learn to behave helplessly. With repetition of this behavior over time, people who allow themselves to fall victim to this condition won't right their situation even when there is an opportunity in front of them to do so.

I find it fascinating to think that situations we encounter in our early years can have dramatic effects on how we problem solve circumstances years later. As you sit there and think about this condition, you may be able to think of instances in your past that interfere with you being the best person you can be, today. I know I can.

We have to remember that we all have the power to affect change in the world around us. Do you think the difference in wildly successful entrepreneurs is that they know how to channel that energy? I do.

Have you ever met people who can walk into a crowded room and the whole room brightens in a positive light? Other people are naturally drawn to those people. What's more, great ideas gravitate toward them and nothing seems impossible.

The ability to affect change positively and help people believe in you and your visions (whether it's a sketch of a small planter for a residential customer or a vision of a huge landscape project for an industrial plant) is a sure path to success."

Some people feel that the world effects them and they are powerless to do anything about it. Others feel like they effect the world and they have the power to change things. We all have the power to change things if we allow ourselves to be positive and think we can.

It is very possible the vast majority of people in our society feel powerless to change anything. This is absolutely something we learn from our interactions within our society and it could very well be explained as 'Learned Helplessness.'

Why do some people want to be an employee? Why do some want to be a boss? Why do some want to be owners? Do they think they can do it or can't do it? Maybe they simply don't care about anything and a weekly paycheck is all they want?

Success is within the reach of everyone who is willing to learn and then do. There will be those who feel they can do nothing and they won't take the time to read and learn. However, there will be those who want it all and want to learn as much as possible. They will be the ones who find much success. Remember you don't have to allow your past experiences to effect your future plans. When the time comes to act, which path will you choose?"

A bigger lawn care business is not necessarily better.

If only we could look into a crystal ball and see our future. Did what we dream of come true or did that dream turn into a nightmare. When you are getting your lawn care business started, you wouldn't think your original plans and goals may lead you straight off a cliff, but you would be surprised.

Reading the stories of others on the Gopher Lawn Care Business Forum really can awaken you to what can go wrong in the business world. When you can see what has happened to others around you who may be ahead of you, it gives you a chance to pause and then reflect for a moment. If you can learn from others' experiences, there is a better chance for you to find a successful outcome they couldn't.

A new lawn care business owner shared with us just such an experience I hope will make you think. He wrote "I recently moved to Florida from New Jersey where I owned a gas station/auto repair business. I was very busy and pretty much burned myself out and was hating life. I worked 12 to 14 hrs. a day with no end in sight to the headaches. One day I decided I had enough and sold out. Then I moved to Florida, where grass grows 12 months a year.

When I got down here I wanted to start fresh with a new business in a new industry. After speaking with local business owners and other people in the know, I decided their was money in any type of home maintenance service. I next purchased an existing lawn care business because I already had business experience and knew what it took to be successful. I did not want to waste time growing one from scratch and I had some money so this was the best step for me.

The business owner I was referred to had very new equipment, and the customers were all bunched together real nicely so not a lot of travel time was being wasted. This lawn care business owner got too big too fast and decided he had enough. He was an individual with no business experience and lost control of it. That is why he opted for the easy way out..to sell cheaply. After purchasing it, I found it to be a money maker right away.

I am still growing and do not advertise. I prefer to get referrals from existing customers. I have been getting about 1-2 new lawn care accounts a week and have just about all I want. I work alone too. I don't want employees again. Employees are expensive. The number of lawns I would have to take on just to cover the employees is not worth it to me. I have always been a firm believer if you price right and work honestly, the money is there. Remember this… just because you are bigger doesn't mean you are making more money, but you can guarantee you will get more headaches.

I have also found good money to be in the 'extras' of the lawn care business. Upselling such services as hedge trimming, fertilizing, roundup spraying garden areas, and irrigation system maintenance. Every house here has an irrigation system, and they all need work. Either adjustments to the heads are needed or the sprinkler units need to be dug up and reset. It's all great money money $$$$. You just have to look for it.

To find success in this or any other business, you need to stay honest. Look your customer in the eye and explain the work needed. If you do this, the customer will agree to the extra work, maybe not right away, but all seem to come around within a short time.

Another secret I learned was to keep Wednesdays open. This gives me a recovery day from rain or a day to do an 'add-on' job for customers in a very timely manner. I do the same with Saturdays as well. I work 1/2 day on lawns as needed, but that leaves time for extras or lawn mowing down time recovery if needed elsewhere along my mowing route. If there are any jobs to catch up on, I go home and relax and have a nice weekend. I DON'T WORK SUNDAYS!

I could keep going on but what I found was this was a great decision. Buy and existing lawn care business and start making money right away. Then let the business buy equipment as you feel you need."

Lawn care business start up mistakes and solutions.

Most every new lawn care business owner is going to mess up on a few things. The way they handle mistakes can make the difference between being able to stay in business for the long haul or losing your customers too soon. One new lawn care business owner got on the Gopher Lawn Care Business Forum and shared with us some of the early mistakes he made and how he was able to resolve them.

He wrote "early on I tended to underbid my lawn mowing jobs, but things got better once I figured I wanted to get $25.00 per hour for my labor on any odd jobs plus cover my operating expenses. As far as materials such as fertilizers and sprinkler hardware, I try to keep a 30% markup (to cover my time and gas money). If I'm not sure of how long a job will take, I just add an extra hour or two on to the bid and then if I get done quicker, I charge less and look like a hero. Since I started handling my estimates this way, everything got easier. Now I just try to keep it simple and follow this basic rule, 'don't be greedy....the greedy become the needy.'"

What advice do you have for other new lawn care business owners when they are looking to figure out how to price the average lawn mowing job?

Also what suggestions do you have on how best to upsell to the customer other services?

"My only advice is for a new lawn care business owner to remember that you are going to make mistakes. You are going to under price some jobs. You are going to tear up some spots on a lawn. The trimmer is going to get away from you and leave a big half moon dead spot near someone's side of house. It happens. What you need to do is figure how to rectify those situations.

I totally spaced out one time and mowed my first pass on a lawn way too low. I mean low, to the thatch! It looked horrible. I was lucky the way it turned out because I told the customer exactly what happened. Then I went back with some fertilizer that had iron in it to quick bring back the green. I asked the customer to set the irrigation to heavy watering. A week later we were all good.

Remember to BE HONEST and don't penalize the customer for your mistakes!

As far as upselling a job I first look to see what needs to be done. A while back I learned one great trick that always seems to work. Don't act like you are trying to sell a job. Get a hold of the customer and show them what you see that needs attention. Tell them what could happen if it doesn't get fixed. Give them some breathing space by saying something to the effect of 'it doesn't need to be done right away, but you should attend to it in the near future. When you are ready, let me know and we'll figure out the best course of action.'

THIS ALWAYS WORKS. Why? Because it makes them feel as if you are not trying to sell them the work for your own personal gain only. Instead it comes across as just you looking out for their property and their best interest. I'd say 80% of the time you have that job before you leave their property because you didn't try rushing or pressuring the customer. They tend to feel more comfortable in your approach. 15% of the time you'll get the job within a couple weeks. Only with the last 5% will you feel you can't win them all.

Be honest and don't try to force or pressure something on a customer. Fess up to your mistakes. The customer may not like what you did, but at least they know you are fixing your mistake and grass always grows back."

Do you have the right stuff to start your lawn care business.

Going from being an employee to starting your own lawn care business can appear to be a daunting challenge. As an employee you don't so much have to find the work as you have to do the work. Many of the day to day business issues are dealt with by the business owner. As an employee, you simply need to be on time, get the job done and collect your paycheck at the end of the week. But what about when you want to make that jump from employee to owner. Will you be successful? Do you have what it takes? That is what a new lawn care business owner was interested in knowing when he wrote us on the Gopher Lawn Care Business Forum.

He said "I'm looking to start my own lawn service and snow plowing business and am in need of some good business tips. I've always had the thought in the back off my head of becoming an entrepreneur, but when it came up I always told myself it wasn't something that I was cut out to do. I have mowed lawns and snow plowed for another lawn service for about 7 years and have always had a passion for it. Lately I had been working with an excavating outfit and recently got laid off due to a lack of work and nothing seemed to be coming down the road. So with all this free time now, I figured if I was ever going to do this, now would be the time.

I always considered myself a 9 to 5er with paychecks on Fridays!! I never thought I could be the businessman as well as the grunt worker. I still don't think that I have all the requirements to be the best at it. My people and sales skills aren't where they need to be either. But I am a firm believer in, if you want something, you have to fight for it and make it happen. So I am ready for anything I can get my hands on. I have been talking to everyone I can talk to and trying to get as much information as I can get before I make a huge investment. I am strongly considering taking a night class at my local community college in business management. Believe me, there are still those lingering thoughts about not being able to do this, but I know I have to get past them.

Trying to keep my head on straight with all of this has been tough. I've got a good friend who is a business owner and about to graduate with his associates degree in business management. He is trying to teach me some valuable information on business operations. I think it's doing more harm than good though in a way. There are so many things to consider when starting a business it makes my head spin. All the licensing, insurance, overhead costs, weekly costs, knowing how much it costs to run my equipment each day, week, and year. How much to figure for equipment depreciation, replacement cost. etc etc. It's enough to drive a person mad.

With all of that said, do I have the right stuff to start my own lawn care business or am I just woefully unprepared?"

As a new business owner, you can't let any of that freak you out. Anything you do that is new, always has the potential of being overwhelming but if you take it in small bites, you can get through it all, step by step.

Getting insurance is as simple as a phone call. Getting a business license is a trip to your local county court house or town hall. Figuring out your operating costs is as simple as taking your total monthly costs and divide that number by the total number of hours you plan on working in that month.

The toughest part you will probably find with everything is attracting new customers. Going from a worker to a salesman, which is what you will become as a business owner, tends to be difficult. Especially for those who aren't extroverts.

To make it easy on yourself early on, promote your business to people you know. Try to get some friends or family members signed up as customers. Use that experience to build up your confidence and then reach out further to neighbors who live in your area. Work on building up referrals from the small group of customers you initially get. As you go, you will find it easier to talk about your business and to sign up more customers.

Don't expect it all to happen overnight because it won't. Slow and steady will win you the race in the long haul. If you are wondering whether or not you have the right stuff to get started, you do. Just remember to take your business building in a step by step fashion. Don't let the setbacks stop you. We all have set backs. Those who succeed, realize set backs are simply momentary and will be overcome.

I thought because I was a great landscaper people would call. I thought wrong.

It's fascinating the lessons learned by new lawn care business owners who leave their full time jobs to go off on their own and start their own business. A member of the Gopher Lawn Care Business Forum shared with us some of the issues he ran into when he got started. He wrote "It's one thing to manage a business for someone but it's definitely another to own a business. I thought that because I was a great landscaper, people would just call. I thought wrong. I now have an interactive website and advertise locally in the community papers. I am trying to make the community aware of the services that I offer."

I think many employees of lawn care businesses tend to not realize how difficult it is to find work. They are normally told where the job is and what they need to do when they get there but rarely are they involved with the sales process. That tends to be where the magic happens. A lawn care business owner who is a good salesman, can find much success in the industry where a quiet more introverted business owner may struggle a lot more to get attention.

When I asked this lawn care business owner to share more of the lessons he learned as he started his own business and how it differed from working for another lawn care company he responded "I have learned that profit is arbitrary. When I managed a concrete, grading, and landscape business for someone else, he had set prices that we went by. The owner would approve our proposals and negotiate with us on the indicated bid price before we even took it to the customer. In this case it was some very large home builders. He had numbers he did not want to go below.

I learned from him that in order to grow I needed to have systems in place that would allow any person with reasonable landscape experience to deliver the same results every time the customer was visited. By this I mean an employee handbook that employees can refer. The previous company I worked for used sub contractors mainly. It was hard to train them on the companies policies because they came and went faster than any company employees would.

I learned that owning my own business means that I am wearing all the hats. I am the Sales Rep, I am the Estimator, I am the Production Manager, I am the Account Controller, I am the Labor, and I am the Marketing Director (the most important when just starting out). I am going to have to learn to do all of these things and develop a system. When that position has been mastered and I have it detailed out I will be able to hire someone to fill that position. They will be able to perform it how I want them to. To succeed as a landscape business owner you have to be a good business person first and then a landscaper second.

I am surprised at how difficult it was to get any publicity for my business. My marketing plan started out as flyers at banks with cardholders and calling the local newspapers to tell them about my business. I wanted an article on the business.....I guess I wasn't too compelling. It's a numbers game totally. I now advertise in a local paper with a large distribution. When new customers call, I always ask - How did you hear about us? I want to track my advertising to see where I am wasting my money.

If you are just starting out like me, with your own landscape business, I would recommend you do not ever skimp on quality or communication. Your first big customers will either make you or break you, and have a great referral program. I have overcome sales objections by simply mentioning my referral program to clients. Sell yourself. Prepare for it like an interview. Have a script ready for phone calls. Be the solution to their landscape concerns. The hardest part is done when They Call YOU. You are the professional. Most people are overwhelmed by their landscape issues. Let them know, you know exactly what to do, how to do it, and why to do it."

Lawn care business lessons from a 20 year veteran.

If you have been in the lawn care business for 20 years, you must be doing something right. That is how many years this member of the Gopher Lawn Care Business Forum has been in the business for. I had an opportunity to talk with him and learn some of his secrets that have kept him in the game for so long and I think you will really benefit from them.

I asked, 20 years in the lawn care business is a long time! Do you feel you were able to learn a lot from them? Do you have a top 5 list of lessons you learned about running a lawn care business? If so, what would be on that top 5 list?

He responded "I would say that of all the things I learned, here is a top 5 list of what I now use as a standard formula. This is how I approach every job.

1. The customer is always right.
2. While the job will never be perfect, when finished it should be as close to perfect as possible.
3. This is one whose benefit you will see at the end of the year. On purchasing materials, set a goal on each job to try and save 10% and during the job try to save 10% more. You have to think a little more, but I'm telling you it works.
4. Volume, when you go into a neighborhood, you should always think about owning it, even if it just starts with one street.
5. Overhead costs should be viewed monthly. The economy has changed, and a lot of contractors are one step away from the curb on any given day. Don't be one of them."

What is the logic behind the 10% rule? So for instance if you were doing a landscape job that required 10 bushes, would you try and only purchase 9?

"The theory in it is if you save 10% on each job, whether it be materials, labor, having materials delivered, working late, etc. you will end up saving money. Every contractor out there can look at every job from the previous year and say 'if I did that differently I would have saved an extra $100.00.' If you do that 20 times in a year, that's a $2,000.00 savings at the end of the year."

What is your suggestion to practically do this? Should you first figure out what you need for a job and then go through it and total it up. Then say, how can I cut 10% from these costs and go with that?

When you look back at jobs you have done, were there places you almost always could save money on? If so, what areas stood out?

"I have found having materials delivered is a big savings. It saves not only on time and fuel, but also wear & tear on the vehicles. When I have a large planting job, I fax the list of materials needed to 3 suppliers, to see who offers me the best price. This always saves money. I also post left over materials on craigslist for free. It is a great way to save money at the landfill, usually this is helpful on hardscape jobs, where there is always a 1/4 pallet left over. People reading craigslist will usually show up an hour after posting to pick the items up."

Is it ever worthwhile at all to charge for these left overs or is it just better to get rid of them?

"Unless you are going to continuously use the same materials, I suggest to just get rid of them. There's no way to order an exact amount of pavers, so if you finish with a 1/4 pallet left over, home run, just give the rest away to someone who wants them."

What is your suggestion on how best to go about owning a neighborhood? And do you mean for lawn care maintenance or other services?

"The only way to own a neighborhood is by offering lower prices. But since your dealing in volume, all you have to do is keep going from house to house without the unloading, loading, and driving time. The more houses you mow in a neighborhood, the more they will call you for other services."

My business got too big and I shut it down. Where I went wrong.

Most every new lawn care business owner has the goal of creating the biggest lawn care business that ever existed. Along that journey, many things can go wrong. Here is one business owner's story about what happened to him. Maybe the lessons he learned on his business adventure will help you avoid the same issues. This is what he shared with us on the Gopher Lawn Care Business Forum.

He wrote "I had a lawn service business about 12 years ago and have done different things since. Lately I have been driving a truck. I don't like being away from home and was thinking about the business again. I had since moved from where I originally had my business so I will have to start from scratch not having any of my original customers around.

You might be wondering why I would simply walk away from a business that I had started and poured my heart and soul into for many years. I guess the simple answer to it is that I got too big too fast and went in too many directions. I started mowing, then tore out someone's landscape and re-installed it with new design and next thing you know it I was getting lots of landscape installs and design projects. I never really felt comfortable doing it and had to learn as I went. I just didn't seem to be able to say no.

At my breaking point, I had many landscape projects going and lots of yards. I just got completely overwhelmed. When a really good job offer came up I guess I decided it would be simpler to just work for someone else and I sold the business.

Now I am living in another state and not sure how business is here. My plan is to restart the business and keep it simple. I am going to just focus on maintenance.

Here are some of the mistakes I made during start up.

When I first started, I had little experience with planting and installing landscapes. I wanted to start maintenance only. When someone asked me to put a garden in, I agreed and started reading some books as I did it. The project came out pretty well so I started getting into it more and more. Meanwhile my advertising was kicking in for maintenance and I was getting accounts too.

What I learned from all that was to pick something and stick with it at first and resist going in too many directions. Keep it simple. Start with basic equipment and focus on advertising the services you decided on. Once you are comfortable with a steady cash flow, then if you want to learn something new, go ahead and offer it to your existing customers. They will be more forgiving if you mess up. Later advertise those services to the general public.

After working on a few projects you should feel comfortable and need to hire a trustworthy person or two. I took things on way too fast and was always freaking out because I didn't have any confidence in what I was doing. Basically I was trying to fake it till I made it.

I went through a lot of consumer grade equipment that first season. I remember running to a big box store in the middle of a mowing job to grab another mower. By the end of the season I had to finally replace all my equipment with commercial grade equipment. I lost a lot of money doing it that way. This time around I will start with commercial grade equipment.

I was always stressed by having to replace and fix cheap equipment and needing help before I could afford it. I spread myself out too thin. That caused me to burn through my profits. By end of first year I had a lot of good equipment and a new truck but had monthly payments to make with no money in the bank.

A job sounded easier, so I sold everything. I am now sorry I did that. I should have told my customers I'm only doing lawns by myself and started over. I am nervous about trying to start now as we are well into the season. It's so hot now the grass is barely growing. I am unemployed and don't want to drive a truck and really want my business again.

Here are some of the tricks I learned.

The best thing I ever did was to get friendly with the local nurseries that didn't offer landscape services. I asked them to recommend me and they certainly did. There was one nursery in particular that most of my business came from. Even if someone bought a tree, they would need someone to plant it for them. Then once I was there I could pick up the yard maintenance from them as well. Upsells were very important. Get your foot in the door with a small job and look around for more services you could offer.

The only other advertising I did was an ad in the local paper, which also worked pretty good. From there, the rest of my jobs came from word of mouth. The trick to being successful with word of mouth advertising is to always 'do what you say you will do and add a little more.' Even if it takes longer to do or the customer is a pain in the butt. Impress whoever you get and word of mouth advertising will just happen.

In the end, you have to scale up your management skills as your business grows. You need to grow with your business and rise above it. Watch your cash flow and make sure you are profiting. Don't let yourself get stressed out because that will lead to burn out.

Once you get to the burnout phase, your business will suffer and you may be looking to sell out like I did.

Steady business growth should be a life long goal. Take growth on slow and steady. In the long run you will benefit from it."

How my lawn care business finally found traction.

It seems some lawn care businesses can find traction at a certain point and take off while others continue to flounder. Why is this? A member of the Gopher Lawn Care Business Forum shared with us how his business finally started to take off and what he did to help.

He wrote "The season just recently started and already I am busy as hell. It's going to be a long season. I have a lot of new lawn care clients signing on and I am dropping the slow payers & pain in the ass clients from last year.

Last year I lost a ton of vacant rental properties I was maintaining in the previous year through a couple property management companies, not because I lost the account but because most of the rentals had tenants. That kinda sucked. However, I gained a bunch of new year round lawn care clients who signed contracts with me. I did more landscape design & install work, More trimming, pruning, and added fertilization as a service.

I actually was cutting a few less lawns per week than in the year prior but was doing more volume of work from each existing customer. So by taping into my current client base I was able to increase revenues significantly over my previous year's figures.

I think some guys fail to get their lawn care business off the ground because of poor business management and going about their business the wrong way. If you try to be the cheap 'budget' service provider, you'll go broke. There is always somebody cheaper, customer loyalty sucks that way. You (hopefully) realize you are not making money so you speed up and then quality suffers. Customers are mad that the quality stinks, you're mad because the money stinks. Nobody is happy and the neighbors certainly aren't going to hire you.

Then what you do next is figure you need more clients and since people aren't hiring their lousy service at $20 bucks a cut they need to drop it to $15 a cut right? WRONG! If you do that, you're an idiot and you'll be working at McDonald's by mid August. Thanks for stopping by the industry! Don't come back.

Instead of going that route, it's very important that you provide a quality service at a fair rate…. Be reliable and your business will grow."

I think this is brilliant! What led to offering this? Was it just that your customers were asking for more or were you looking for it and promoting them as upsells?

I think a lot of newer lawn care businesses aren't going to see this, but do you feel that there is a higher profit margin in offering these add on or upsell services, than there is in mowing? So in a sense does offering the mowing services, open the door to selling more services to your clients?

"Well I did actively work at upselling add on services to existing lawn care customer. Yes, almost anything is more profitable than just mowing, however mowing is what keeps you in front of your clients all the time. In a sense it is a necessary loss leader.

Once you serve a client for a while, answer their questions and inform them of any problems with their lawn, or plants, or trees, they tend to trust you more when you recommend another service should be performed. It all adds up, even little trim and prune jobs… $25 for that tree, $30 for those bushes etc. it all adds up to another $100/day = an extra $2,000 + for the month. Now add a couple little landscape jobs in each month. A couple fertilization jobs and you are adding $3-5k each month on top of your lawn revenues. Not counting the occasional complete landscape overhaul."

Because lawn care is highly competitive, is it ever worthwhile taking on a customer if you feel that the mowing end of it will break even at best? In hopes they can be upsold too?

Do you find all customers can be upsold or should you only keep customers that you can upsell to and get rid of the others?

"I am not interested in doing anything at a break even rate. I really don't need the practice at this point. Not everyone will buy the upsell type services and that's ok. I don't drop customers for not buying other upsell services. My point is that lawn care can keep you in business and keep you from starving day to day, the other services turn better profit typically."

Great points to keep in mind when you are looking to make your lawn care business grow. If you go down the cheap mowing path, you can see how it can become a death spiral for your business. Instead of being cheap, provide a quality service and build trust. That seems to be the best way to upsell customers on more lawn care and landscape services.

Why I left the lawn care business.

Entrepreneurs are people and people sometimes just get burned out. They get bored. They don't find the results they were hoping to find or they simply want to try something new. There are many reasons why business owners give up on their businesses. In this discussion from the Gopher Lawn Care Business Forum, one business owner shares with us why he left the lawn care business. Maybe some of these insights will help you with your business plans and goals. Knowing why others quit or gave up can help you avoid those situations.

He wrote "I left the lawn care business. The main reason for leaving is the 45 lawn care contracts I had. There was a lot of work and I tried hiring someone on to help me. I ended up having three different employees and all of them were fired for stupidity or not showing up. All of those contracts were for one customer. What I learned from that is don't put all your eggs all in one basket as they say. The property maintenance contracts were all for one client and the agreement wasn't the best for me in the end. I had under bid the properties. Gas prices on the rise didn't help either.

I am now kicking around the idea of starting up another company again but after learning how to bid jobs and learning more from other lawn care business owners, it seems that it would be hard to make any money just mowing. Next time I will try to find a niche to make a better profit and go for it.

I love working for myself and wouldn't want it any other way."

Another lawn care business owner shared "It's not impossible to make money in the lawn care business. It's like anything. It's not chance or luck, it's basically having the right mind set in order to create fresh strategies to progress.

It's hard to make money on EVERY job you bid when you are just starting out. You need to allow yourself some time to learn and grow. Don't expect everything to work right the first time out and don't jump into contracts right away and lock yourself in potentially bad bids for a year. You gotta play your cards right in order to achieve success.

For instance I honestly didn't think I'd be able to triple my client base this season. I wanted to badly, but I didn't want to get my hopes up. I hunkered down and focused on the basics. I took my truck out an chatted with every person I saw on the road. Handed out business cards. Added signs to my truck and trailer and I found with a little extra kick in the butt, you can get what you want.

It's all about the drive you have. Personally I had no drive when I was in school. I didn't understand the future school would provide me with. From that experience I learned I needed to take charge and do things on my own. I needed to become self reliant.

Since then I have never been happier. I wanted to learn what I wanted to learn, not what everyone else was. I found an inner drive to keep me going. When I wake up in the morning I ask myself what I want and then I go for it!

If I want 50+ lawn care customers, once I leave my driveway in the morning I then am on a mission and it's as simple as that. I'm not saying I have the most drive out of everybody but I have to admit, I have yet to feel like I am giving it EVERYTHING I've got, so there is quite some room for improvement.

The more comfortable I get with myself and the more confidence I build, I find that getting clients is a lot easier. I used to just make flyers to promote my business and I knew they didn't work but I still handed thousands out anyway. That was me just being lazy. I admit it.

But the thing is, if I wanted more customers, I had to ask myself what's really stopping me? Is it a level of comfort I'd have to sacrifice? Of course! In order to achieve, you've gotta get a little uncomfortable. Instead of just handing out flyers and sticking them in mail boxes, you gotta meet people and get to know them.

You have it in you to answer almost any problem you would experience in this industry. We all have what it takes to succeed. We have to go out there, experiment, and give ourselves time to adjust and learn from our mistakes. Then we will grow."

Average lawn care business start up costs.

One of the big questions I tend to hear from entrepreneurs who are considering starting up a lawn care business is, how much will it cost to start up my new business? Costs can vary greatly depending on how big you go or how cheap you have to keep it but I thought if I could show you at least what four business owners thought of this topic, it would give you a pretty well rounded answer. To review more start up costs visit this discussion on the Gopher Lawn Care Business Forum.

* One lawn care business owner shared:

Well for me taking into consideration I was mostly a landscaping business:

Truck $5000
Trailer $1000
Advertising $120
Equipment $700 (rakes, shovels, wheel barrows, etc.)
Truck insurance $300/yr
Company registration $100
Business insurance $700/yr
Truck registration $120
Trailer registration $70

So about $8000 in total.

* A second lawn care business owner shared:

Used pick up $1500
Used 21" mower $75
Used string trimmer $50

Used blower $50
Used edger $50
Business license $80
1 mil. liability insurance $478 (yearly)
Truck insurance $150 (monthly)
Gallon of 2 stroke oil $10
5 gallon fuel can $10
2 gallon fuel can $8
7 gallons of fuel $19 (89octane)

So roughly $2,480 could put you in business legally and grow it from there.

   * A third business owner started on the cheap and shared how he did it.

I started by using the car I own and pay on monthly. I use the trunk for my lawn care equipment. It sucks but it's better than nothing.
So....

Used car-$60.00/week
22" mower $75 (bought off season) in season its $150
String trimmer (FREE) giving from a friend. Sells for $70
New blower $100
Car insurance $18.75/week
2 gallon fuel can $5 (mower)
1 gallon fuel can $2.50 (Trimmer) 40:1 ratio oil/gas
1 gallon fuel can $2.50 (blower) 50:1 ratio oil/gas

So roughly $400-600 put me in business but I still need to go legal and most of the equipment I had already for my own yard. I just use it since I already have it. When I get more money I'll buy what I need to expand with cash only, so there is not borrowing.

   * A fourth lawn care business owner wrote:

Lawn Mower: $1,500.00
Trimmer: $500.00
Blower: $200.00
Marketing Material: $250.00
Cell Phone: $100.00
Gas Can: $20.00
Mix Can: $20.00
Trimmer Cord: $30.00
Eye Protection: $15.00
Grass Can: $40.00
Garbage Bags: $30.00
Rake: $30.00
Tarp: $15.00
Garden tools: $50.00

Total: $2,800.00

This does not include truck payments since I already owned it.

Excited, unsure, too much, not ready, all mixed together!!!

What would you do if you received a phone call from a local landscaping company and they offered to give you all their lawn care customers? Would you find this to be a curse or a blessing? At first glance it may seem like a fantastic opportunity to jump on, however there are many issues to consider. This is a situation a member of the Gopher Lawn Care Business Forum was facing when he wrote us about it and asked how much growth is helpful and how much is just too much?

He wrote "I just got a call from another landscaping company in town who has been doing yard care as well as landscaping. He wanted to know if I would be interested in taking on his yard care clients as he has decided to concentrate on landscaping only. He is willing to turn them over to me, however I am not in the position of being able to handle them all. It would increase my client base by 200%, which would require hiring guys. The extra work would be awesome, but here are my issues.

    * Hiring guys might mean a constant rotation of employees. There have been a few lawn care businesses I have heard comment that they have trouble maintaining employees. I am not sure if the reward is worth the headache.

    * Secondly, I have built my business on quality. In the years I have been operating, I have gotten the reputation of being the company in town that does some of the best work. Not being able to be totally hands on might cause issues with the quality of workmanship.

    * This could be a big break for me and be a chance to build on what I have started. It could turn into me being able to take some

more time off once the new employees know what and how I want things done.

I have to add that I also find this somewhat scary. Too many lawn care companies have grown too big, too fast and in the end it ruins them."

This is a very interesting topic. In the past, on the forum we have talked about how 20% growth each year is a ceiling you shouldn't go above. Can you add enough customers to hit that mark and no more?

How many customers would you ideally like to add now and still feel comfortable with your growth? What's your current workload and workforce?

One other thing to keep in mind is, adding employees is no guarantee you will be able to take some time off. Managing your staff to ensure quality and performance will no doubt, take more time than you initially thought.

"I've been handling 27 clients to date by myself. This other landscaping business owner is offering me 47 new lawn care customers. We didn't discuss whether I was buying them, he basically wanted to know if I would be interested in taking them on. I got the impression he just wanted to make sure they were going to have someone looking after them, so I would guess they were free.

I think this is why it can be scary. I have had some growth this year already. I have been wanting to pick up about 5 more clients in addition to the new ones I got this spring already. He however wants to make sure this group of 47 would be looked after. I'm hesitant to even take a few more additional ones on. I guess it would depend on what he was charging them and if I could find enough help to make it pay.

Realistically, I was very happy with the growth that I had already achieved and wasn't looking to take on any more customers. I can understand him not wanting to leave his clients in a bind, I would feel the same way, but this may be way too much growth for me."

Maybe the best way to go about this would be to contact him, express to him your concerns and see what kind of deal you can work out.

"That's exactly what I did. I chatted with him tonight and told him I would take on one group of his clients, 13 in total and all in one location. After some discussion, he told me what he was charging them and I can live with it for the summer. I might raise the rates next year just to get a slightly higher profit margin. I figure I can handle them with just one additional employee and basically these customers will pay his wages for the summer season."

UPDATED INFO…

Two months later he wrote "the 13 lawn care customers I had agreed to take on did not happen. A new guy in town came along and scooped them up before I was given their names. From what the other company told me, he offered them a lower price. I have seen his work since and let's just say 'you get what you pay for.'

I have picked up several new clients from that company as he has been referring them to me. It has worked out reasonably well. I am still adding clients but at a slower rate which is more in my comfort zone.

The employee I added is working out reasonably well, but I am finding I have to constantly remind him of little things now and again. He fixes them and things go well for a few weeks then he starts getting sloppy again. I figure this is just standard employee management.

In the end, I am glad I did not take on all those extra customers. I prefer growing at a comfortable pace."

When is enough, enough? When should I get out?

I think most new lawn care business owners will go through a time when they sit for a moment and really question what it is they are doing. Are they making enough? Do they have enough customers? Is this business of theirs' going to work or is it failing and they just haven't accepted it yet? That is what one member of the Gopher Lawn Care Business Forum wondered when he asked "I'm sure a lot of people ask this question, when is enough, enough already? Is enough, enough when you just don't enjoy it anymore? When it gets harder to make ends meet? How long must I be on the end of the losing side before I give up?

I have been tossing this very idea around a lot lately in my head. My personal situation is as follows, I am really not making any money. I am staying in the black but just barely. After gas and other expenses I may have like $5 per month extra that I can't even touch but rather must put in the bank just in case another piece of equipment breaks down. Right now with our weather I only have one regular client who only gets his lawn mowed once per month for $40. So my business is taking in $40 per month right now. I am starting to just not enjoy it anymore. I figure that's it I quit. I have a few other business ideas that I am thinking about experimenting with, so maybe I will quit and focus more on them but for some reason I keep going with my lawn care business. I say I quit but then tomorrow I get right back at it. It strange to me, I feel like I have
1- No money
2- No clients
3- Not enjoying it
4- Far less time with family

I have only been in business for 7 months. So far being under a year old and in a failing economy I am still managing to keep it in the black each month which I guess says a lot for itself. I just figure since this is not my first time at starting a business I should have skipped a lot of the early traps and pulled a profit sooner, I don't know. I guess so long as it stays in the black maybe it's worth hanging onto a little while longer. I feel the clear answer is QUIT but for some reason I just can't. I don't know it's weird.

I guess I shouldn't complain about too much. 7 month after my start up I am making a profit. I am just extremely disappointed on how slow things are going. I am holding down so much right now I know a lone man can't do this forever so I hope to god this being my 2nd year, that this really takes off so I can let go of my day job and finally relax for 3 minutes a week. Right now its just go go go go from 5am until nearly midnight every night 7 days a week. Lawn care is making me so little right now, which is why I believe it has left a bad taste in my mouth. I feel like I have tried everything so far and nothing has worked for me. I understand every situation is different and what works for one won't for another but nothing seems to work for me."

One lawn care business owner said "If you're not succeeding / excelling in this business after 1.5-2 years you might consider getting a job working for someone else."

Another suggested "here is what I recommend for you. After only 7 months, do not give up, you are half way there. However, as a start up you should not be hiring anyone, keep it a solo gig until you can't handle it anymore by yourself. You really should work alone for 1.5-2 years to get the company off the ground before you can hire someone.

Later you can add a part time helper, for one day a week, only when you really need it or you feel yourself burning out. One a month tops, unless you get some big clean up job that requires extra help."

A third lawn care business owner said "when you are new in the business, there is a tendency to think big however, thinking about being a million dollar company after 7 months is a bit absurd. Most companies don't even turn a profit for the first 5 years. I'm sure you've heard of the 5 year business plan.

After enough time, there is no reason a properly run and operated lawn/landscaping company can't become a multi-million dollar a year business. I know of several of them. You are just not going to see it over night or out of most companies.

There are a lot of people in the industry because they can't get a job anywhere else. Because of that, they are not business educated nor do they have any interest in making more than a bare minimum of cash. I am not one of those people, my net income will surpass 6 figures this year. A true entrepreneur should always be striving for more! I will be starting 2 more companies this year also in the service industry. While some might make more money than others, it's foolish to close any business, other than a complete loser. Give it time, work on it and you will see your business grow."

Should you ever accept unprofitable landscaping jobs?

Lawn care business owners are in business to make money. It's plain and simple. But are there ever times when it is alright to accept a lawn care or landscaping job when you know it won't be profitable? Are there any upsides to doing this and if so, what are they? That is what one lawn care business owner questioned on the Gopher Lawn Care Business forum.

He wrote "today I was thinking about the concepts of bidding lawn care jobs. Normally, if a customer does not accept an initial bid price, it's probably better for the lawn care business owner to walk away instead of doing it for an unprofitable price. But there are occasions where you might want to reconsider and accept jobs which you know ahead of time will be unprofitable.

One I can think of is for cash flow issues. Sometimes, a lawn care business owner needs immediate positive cash flow into his business today in order to cover expenses.

A second could be in order to retain employees. Depending on your climate and where you live, many lawn care business owners will lay off employees during winter due to a drop off in the demand for their services. Any employee that is laid off will often find other work and may decide not to come back to work for you in the spring. Accepting some unprofitable jobs might be able to bring you in just enough cash to pay an employee so he won't leave to find other work during winter.

A third reason might be to trim down stock that would go bad over the colder months. For example, lawn seed can be expensive. To reduce cost your costs, you may purchase lawn seed in bulk. If you buy too much seed during the year, you will have a surplus that may last you into winter. If the unused seed is being stored, it may go to waste or possibly take up valuable space in your shop. If winter is coming, you may agree to take on an unprofitable seed job in order to get rid of the excess seed.

Lastly you may find an unprofitable job may bring with it the promise of future work or advertising. This is probably my least advisable reason for taking on unprofitable work. Sometimes a lawn care business owner feels a customer will have more jobs in the future if he will give a really low price on the first job. Before you go ahead and do this, realize it is a dangerous proposition since that extra work often fails to appear.

With all these reasons stated above, I am not advocating you take on unprofitable landscaping jobs. Each job has to be examined on a case by case basis. If you take on too many unprofitable jobs, you will soon find yourself out of business. So, be wary and take on these jobs for specific reasons that you can rationally make sense of."

Another lawn care business owner shared "I would never take on a job if I knew in the very beginning it wasn't a money maker. Sometimes jobs don't turn out the way you thought they would and those become money losing jobs. If this is something that couldn't have been helped, you mark it as a lesson to be learned from and you go over everything in detail about that job 100 times until you find why you lost money on it. Then in the future you can fix it and not make that same mistake twice.

When times are tough, they can be made tougher by taking unprofitable jobs. If it's just labor lost then is it really a losing job? No. It just means you didn't make as much as you wanted to. If you find your family getting hungry then yes I would do a job for less money if labor is all that was involved. If I had to buy materials of any kind for such a job, then no I wouldn't do it."

Should I buy this lawn care business?

Buying an already functioning lawn care business is a way to get started with a bang. The upside to it is you should immediately have cash flow and hopefully a positive cash flow at that. But there are plenty of downsides to it as well. You need to weigh the pro's and con's before you consider buying any lawn care business.

Let's take a look at one lawn care business that a member of the Gopher Lawn Care Business Forum was looking into purchasing. Studying this example may help you if you find yourself in a similar situation.

The new business owner wrote "over the last month or so, my husband and I have decided to start a lawn care business. He currently works at a full time job, but is looking for a more flexible schedule. To do this we only want to replace his current income with the lawn care, but some extra money would be great (especially with 5 kids at home).

I drive a school bus and he would do the same in the winter. So that would help pay the bills during the slow seasons. He has talked for years about wanting to mow in the summer, and I think now is the right time.

The plan WAS for me to get the business going by starting out specializing in edging only (an old friend did that years ago, and she was quite successful at it) and doing the work myself, since my husband still has to keep his job. We would take on a few mowing jobs for my husband to do after work to get it going. Then, if we built up enough income in edging to replace his income, we could add the mowing/maintenance service and try to get 60 or so weekly mowing customers.

Since I am not new to the business arena (having run my own specialty painting/faux finishing business for 7 years) I started networking with some business contacts. By doing this I found a friend of mine who owns a contracting business had purchased a used lawn care outfit a few years ago (truck, trailer, mowers, equipment, plow, yard vacuum, etc.) to supplement his services. He has since decided to get out of it. He found that after the expense of paying someone to do the work, he wasn't making much money.

He's including the client list, will include marketing the business in a newsletter for 1 year to help me out, and will send any calls for business to me. His truck already has nice logo and I like the name of the business, so we would probably keep that.

I am currently waiting to hear back on the cost, but he said it wouldn't be much since all the equipment is good, but used. He even said would take payments since we are friends.

Any words of caution, things I should look for, when considering jumping at this chance? Or, would I be better off starting from scratch, and keep going down the same road I was headed?"

One lawn care business owner responded "well the fact that the guy is willing to take payments implies that he is relatively confident you can make enough to make the payments and that is a plus. However, if he said he's not making enough to make it worth his while, it's probably not enough for you either. He may be under pricing the jobs or may be managing it poorly. You need to find out which!

If he's under priced and you buy the business & jack up the rates, you may lose a good percentage of his current customers. You need to find out if his current customers are paying per service or contracted monthly?

Another big unknown here is the cost. It's impossible to even weigh this opportunity out until you know the cost. How much equipment does he have and what it's worth? How many customers does he have? You said a snow plow is included but you said you want extra income in the summer only. If that is the case, there will be equipment you don't need or want as you'll be driving a school bus in the winter. Also you need to check if he includes plowing in the winter time for the current customers. Would you be locked into having to provide those services like it or not?

When I was getting started, I looked at other businesses for sale too and ultimately decided to start from scratch with no loan over my head. The one business I looked at had about $10k in used equipment. Plus he had about 130 customers that paid per cut & no contracted customers. I decided against it because he wanted $60k for the biz.

I thought to myself, well many customers are going to be loyal to the guy who's been servicing them so when a new owner comes in, I figured it was fair to guestimate I might lose 10-15% just because I wouldn't be the same guy they were used to. I also knew most companies on average get lazy & do a lousy job & or become unreliable. So I figured that I could build my business from the ground up by doing a great job every time, offering competitive rates & better service.

So that's what I've done so far & it's working for me. I was able to buy most of the equipment with some cash from my savings. A used trailer, new trimmers, edgers, blowers, chain saws, pole saw & hedge trimmer. I financed what I couldn't purchase in cash, which was a new commercial mower.

Instead of 60k overhead I only have about 1/8th of that debt. In less than a year my business is about half what his was already. Every situation is different and I wish all the best of luck to you!

But keep in mind, you will have it easier than me. I had no other income and had to start from customer #1 & build it up. Luckily you are just looking to supplement your income, so this process could be easier for you."

Self re-newing lawn care contracts a good idea?

Do you find it difficult to keep your lawn care customers from year to year? At the end of the year are you in panic mode trying to get all your customers to re-sign back up with you the next year? It seems some lawn care business owners have this problem while others do not. So what is the best way to handle such a problem? That is the question a lawn care business owner wondered about when he wrote us on the Gopher Lawn Care Business Forum.

He wrote "I realize that everyone will handle this situation completely different but here in the south, lawn care is year round. During the winter months, mowing may slow a bit and be about half the frequency (bi-weekly), but I keep busy all year. My question though is, what's the best way to keep my lawn care customer base along with me into the next year?"

One lawn care business owner shared "I use a lawn care contract that handles this problem. A while back it occurred to me that if I have to go to each client & point out 'hey you're done with 12 months! Thank you, now would you like to sign up for the next 12?' It raises the question, 'Do I want to continue?' Why wave this flag? Why make something that is a non-issue suddenly an issue?

When you sign up for cell phone service for 2 years they don't call you up on the first day of year 3 and say 'do you want phone service tomorrow' do they? No, they just continue to provide their service at the same rate & everyone is happy. They have already had you for 2 years & covered the initial cost of the phone, so now most likely you will continue under the same contract until your phone breaks.

Our situation in the lawn care industry is similar but different. In my case, I have my clients sign a lawn care agreement and here is how I have it worded. My customers are required to pay each month in advance on the 1st.

This agreement will continue in effect as long as both parties are satisfied. To cancel service, the client must provide written notice 30 days in advance of intended cancel date. If you do not wish to have us continue a 2nd year simply notify us & do not pay the 13th monthly invoice. Otherwise the 12 month cycle will automatically restart with the same conditions as the 1st year."

Another lawn care business owner shared "with cell phone contracts, at least here, it's month to month after the initial term. One can word into their agreement the contract will automatically renew for a period of 12 months unless 90 days notice is given however, once again, at least here you can't enforce the automatic renewal in court should you have to go that route. I understand laws can very greatly depending on the area you live, so it's worth checking your local laws before you do this.

Instead of contracts, why not focus on superior service? I personally see my interactions with clients more as relationships rather than just a check/payment etc. I send a letter to my clients every quarter updating them on what I and the company are up to. When these letters go out, I usually receive quite a few emails back.

Having said that, we all lose a customer for whatever reason from time to time. But I know the work is there and will continue to be there so long as you treat your customers well and do the best job you can. I don't tend to concern myself so much about them leaving at the end of a contract, term or year. Focus on quality at a fair price and the rest will take care of itself."

Quality vs. Quantity in the lawn care industry.

There is a delicate balance that a lawn care business owner must consider when they create their business plan. Will they be going for a quantity of customers and profit little per each customer or will they go for quality and profit more per customer but have less of them? You only have so much time to work during your day and the more time you spend per lawn, the better it may look but the less customers you can service per day. You can charge more per lawn and profit more when you do a better job, but there is always that allure with beating your competitors price and going for quantity.

This topic was discussed on the Gopher Lawn Care Business Forum when a member wrote "I think success in this business has a lot to do with the balance of quality vs. quantity of work.

If you shoot for the quantity, you need to be very efficient and waste no time. That allows you to decrease expenses and price as compared to your competition. In return you will gain clients that are shopping based on price. With this strategy you can have a lot of lower paying customers but in the end make money because of your efficiencies.

On the other hand, if you take the extra time to look at the little things and talk to your customers every now and then, you are providing more quality work. Efficiencies are lower and you will probably have to charge a little more to make as much as the competition. Your niche market will be those customers looking for quality work and are willing to pay the extra bucks per mow which in the end can make you more money than the quantity strategy."

Another lawn care business owner said "Quantity vs. Quality. Mow and Go vs. Stay and Pay …or perhaps a bit of both? I find myself changing it up all of the time, but I mostly lean towards quality (there are exceptions). All of this depends on the situation, client, property. In the lawn care business you really need to adapt.

There are methods to maintain premium quality and still mow 25+ lawns per day. The secret is you need to build routines and be consistent. Once you do that you'll find that your route will run like a well oiled machine.

The fact of the matter is you should never sacrifice quality in order to push your business forward. If you do this you'll find yourself in a decline and you'll never know what happened until it is too late.

Here is an example:

I received a phone call last spring requesting a quote for lawn maintenance. They told me that the company they have been using for the past year shows up with 3 guys. They all hop on machines, fly around, grass is going everywhere, skid marks in their lawn and on their driveway from the mowers, gardens are full of grass and they don't blow anything out so the clippings are everywhere. It was a rant for sure!

So I showed up to the property 1 hour after the initial call. I was surprised to find out that it was a 1.5 acre lot and the lawn was a mess. One of the first questions I always asked was how long does it usually take to mow the lawn? Asking that loaded question gives me tons of info about the previous company and what the client is looking for. From it I found out that it took them 2.5 hours to cut, trim and blow (even though there showed no signs of blowing), and they charged $45.00 per cut.

First of all there is no way that company was making any money with productivity rate of $6.00 per man hour. I laughed in my head.

I quoted the job at $75.00 per mow on a 26 visit contract, which came to $1,950.00 a year. I got the job. It takes us 1 hour to mow, trim and blow.

2 workers x 0.5hrs = 1hr total
$75.00 / 1hr / 2 = $37.50 productivity per man hour

Those are not bad numbers but I would like them to be higher.

So I guess what I am trying to say is that the other lawn care company was not as efficient as mine. They wasted time by not delegating tasks and it took them 1.5hrs longer to mow the lawn. On top of that, they low balled the property to begin with. In the end they lost the job due to quality issues.

You can find efficiencies by doing the job right. Make sure you quote the job to be profitable! Nothing gets my goat more than listening to people say things like 'if I charge less I'll get more customers.'

The biggest thing lacking in the lawn care industry is structure. Anyone has the ability to say 'I'll cut your lawn for $10.00' and you know what? They might get the job and they might get lots of jobs, but in the end quality will fall and clients will realize that they made a wrong choice. Once the customer realizes that, they will be looking for their next lawn care service provider."

How to make sure you get paid from your landscaping jobs.

The first rule you should learn when it comes to running your lawn care or landscaping business is never lose money. The second rule is to not forget the first rule. With that said, many lawn care and landscaping businesses at some time, lose money on a job and some times it is big money. Sure they can underbid on a job and lose money, but the biggest way to lose money, is to not have a system in place that guarantees you will be paid by the customer once the work is complete. If you think not getting paid for a job could never happen to you, think again. It is of the utmost importance on large jobs, that you use some sort of contract and get paid in steps as you complete the work. Otherwise you might find yourself out tens of thousands of dollars.

A lawn care business owner talked to us about his experiences of getting paid for his landscape work on the Gopher Lawn Care Business Forum and I felt it was a very good learning lesson.

He wrote "most builders and developers in my 30 years of experience are in the business for the quick cash. When they are building new homes, their goal is to, get it up, make it look pretty, sell and let the buyer worry about the problems

The number one issue starts many new homeowners in my area find themselves dealing with is drainage and excavation issues. When it comes to excavation, very few excavation companies can read grades and even less do the job right. They slope properties in all sorts of ways that funnel rain water right into a homes basement. Or slope driveways in such a manner that they quickly erode. This is why I am making a killing.

I recently picked up a new driveway landscape project from a homeowner who saw a driveway I built two streets over. He saw my gear at the site, stopped and asked if I would look at his place which I did. I gave him a very rough estimate as this kind of work I bill by the hour. He hired us on the spot with a $15,000 down payment and billed every three days, pro-rata.

My down payment calculations depend on a few variables. These are the issues I take into account when creating a down payment value. I consider the job I will be working on, how my conversation goes with the customer and my feeling of how well we will work together. In general though it usually comes out to 25% of the total job cost. I bill labor and machines at $5,000 every three days. That is to cover 6 guys and three machines, plus profit.

Being paid pro-rata means if you give me a $15,000 job deposit, after 3 days of work I will give you a bill for $5,000. If the job is 10% done at that time, you owe me $5,000 less $1,500 (the $1,500 is 10% of the full deposit) so I require a check for $3,500.00 before any further work is completed. The customer and I agree to all this up front. I have no receivables, never have, never will. I don't want to waste my time tracking down old customers to collect payment. My invoices are presented via email from my software and I will wait for the check or credit card in the morning before work is continued. The customer will also already know where to leave the check so I can find it. I have never had an issue yet using this payment policy.

Any job over $5,000 needs a deposit. I learned a long time ago that things can happen on the payment side and my costs run high when I have that much gear and that many people on a job site.

In short I have to protect myself and this is a perfect way to do it. I am very up front with the client at the start and not one has ever said anything about it to complain. If they did, I would walk. This is a red flag to me and I am in a position where I have so many big jobs available and signed that I don't need to put up with any nonsense. When a customer puts up a red flag, I just go to the next one.

In the past, when I was hungry for money, I tended to take higher risks jobs and generally still got paid but there have been a few times when I haven't. If I am already hungry and I do work and don't get paid, I will be starving. In such situations if you don't be careful you will could find yourself out of business.

So make sure you protect yourself and your business by implementing a payment plan that both you and your customer can agree upon before you start working."

What's keeping your business from growing by leaps and bounds?

If your lawn care business has not been growing as fast as you wanted it to this year, have you taken some time to stop and think about why it hasn't? If after thinking about it, you are still unsure, maybe hearing the story of another business owner who found growth will help you compare and contrast yourself to see what you could potentially be improving on. A member of the Gopher Lawn Care Business Forum shared with us his story of business growth this year.

He wrote "well I have to admit, this year has been a really good one. I'm thinking about buying another truck and hiring two part timers. This time last year I had maybe 5 lawns. This year I have 48 and still averaging a new one every day. I'm getting really behind already, and I'm kind of apprehensive about growing so fast. I know this is a good thing, however I'm feeling gun shy about hiring and purchasing another truck. Granted, it's a good used truck and it's coming from a good friend, and it's only $1,500. He took good care of it, and it will be paid for in cash when I get finished with one landscape job next week, but I am still concerned.

What I would attribute this growth to is 'Quality, Quality, Quality.' When I service a lawn, I do the best I can do and treat it like it was my own mother's lawn. I literally treat each and every customer like they were my own family and I always give them small freebies when I can to make them feel special. Anytime they need something like a few small weeds sprayed in the driveway, or a few small limbs picked up and hauled away, I always do it for them for nothing. I think it makes them feel special and appreciated. I always make time to visit with them and be sincere when I ask them how they are.

My work is always flawless, I never do sloppy work. The clippings are always blown back into the lawn, I never blow grass from the mower or trimmers up against a house or outbuilding or onto the neighbors lawn, and I always keep my lines perfectly straight with the mowers. They pay me to do quality work, and that's exactly what they get, consistently, every time. I've had 100% retention on all my customers because of this, and I have yet to ever lose one because of my work. I tell them up front that I am a professional lawn service and I may not be the cheapest, but my work is the best around.

The way I saw the growth happening was that quality would get me the quantity. I believe that if you do great work, you'll get more customers. I've always been particular about making things look the best, and that's what I do with my lawns.

The way I see it is this: Any moron can mow a yard. It takes a professional to manicure a lawn. I keep my work one step above the other companies.

I'm always paying attention to the ways my competitors mow and trim, and I go one better. When I push mow, I make those lines perfectly straight. When I trim, I never leave a blade of grass standing, and I always turn the trimmer on it's side and edge the sidewalks and curbs on every account. When I blow the clippings, I also blow off their patios and porches, whether they are covered with grass clippings, or just leaves and dirt from them not sweeping. Customers notice this kind of stuff and that's why they seek me out. This ain't just a job, it's a passion and I'm doing it because I want to, not because I have to.

As I need to expand and hire more staff I am concerned about the level of quality my company will be able to perform. At this time, I am having new customers who haven't had their yards mowed yet and they're getting tall and I'm having to schedule them two days ahead to even fit them in. By the time I get there, I have to spend twice as long because I have to literally mow it twice to mulch up the clumps to make it look nice. Another concern of mine is when I hire my employees and I set these guys loose, they won't do as good of a job as I do and I may lose my 100% retention on my customers.

My business has finally taken off but I am going to have to rethink my business plan in order to keep control over all this growth. I can now see how at a certain size, such a business can spin out of control and collapse on itself."

Another lawn care business owner shared "it's great to hear that you are growing that fast! As you expand and take on more liabilities, you may not make as much per location as you used to, however you should still be making a profit.

Growth can be very painful, I went through this last year and it was brutal. This business was supposed to be a company that I could work with my son and maybe one friend at during the summer when he was home from school but it has since grown to a staff of 16.

At one point I found myself being nothing more than an office manager. The amount of paperwork in this company is nuts as we do everything by the book. Long story short I had to take quite a bit of time to get people, processes and polices in place, in order to continue forwards and allow me to free up my time spent in the office. So far this year has been far better because of it."

What I learned about the lawn care business this year.

I asked the members of the Gopher Lawn Care Business Forum, what they learned this year about business as they reflected back. The fall and winter are great times to take a moment and sit back to think about the lessons you learned over the past year. What have these lessons taught you and how can you make next year better. Here is what some of them had to say.

One lawn care business owner said "this was a learning year. I found that door hangers, flyers, posters, and door to door had less than desirable results. As far as marketing results, newspaper ads and having a blog that I got listed on my local city web site was by far the most productive.

I found competing with the competition didn't work. Offering the same services and products they had just left me spinning my wheels.

Differentiating myself from them was the key. I found organic lawn care is much more profitable than mowing. I won't turn down mowing contracts but I don't seek them out anymore. Organic lawn treatments, sod, tilling and re-seeding are what I will concentrate after organic lawn treatments."

A second business owner shared "This past year was a year of learning and revamping the business plan. I wish I knew then and had the equipment I do now when I started.

I was performing various cost break downs with every job we do. Landscaping projects at times was taking me four trips to perform. Two to delivery and two to pick up because of the amount of equipment I needed and the size of my trailer. I average 10 mpg, tops, pulling gear so it really added up. So I bought a 14,000 pound trailer that is 19 feet long, and I can now transport everything in one shot.

I learned there is a limited market for me in mowing which is fine. I have many private divisions and a few residential in my area. They are basically enough to keep one crew going. I have no plans to expand my mowing next year unless it falls in my lap. Instead I have found there is big money in pressure washing, organic spraying, wood cutting, chipping, post hole digging, excavation, and landscaping.

I also determined that using a tractor with a chipper was a very poor choice so I traded them all in for trailer units to free the tractors up where they make a lot more money doing other jobs. Now I simply use one of my ATV's to pull the chipper around the client's site instead of a tractor.

A chipper that attached to the tractor runs around $8,000. The issue is, the most I could get for a tractor and chipper per hour was $45.00, but the tractor on a job site doing loader work or whatever brings in $75.00 an hour. The cost of the tow unit chippers is not cheap as I wanted, diesel with auto feed, so they run close to $22,000 each. There is a very big demand for such chippers as the rental places rent them with a manual feed for $240.00 a day. The problem with a manual feed is that it kills your arms within an hour. With my automatic feeder I simply feed the entire tree. I only chip up to 5″ however it will do 8″ but that should be cut into firewood which we do for $35.00 an hour and split it with a splitter we have for $45.00 an hour.

The tractor is cheap to run however, it could and does bring in a lot more money elsewhere so I now simply load the chipper attached to one of the ATV's on a trailer and take it to the site, staff can then pull it where ever it's required.

Next year I also plan on building septic fields. I am told offering such services is a license to print money and I start my training course on that next week."

A third member said "I learned I needed to invest in more equipment to make more money per man hour. I just recently bought a new Bobcat Toolcat 5600 today from a dealer for snow removal this winter and commercial work this summer. This machine has the potential to utilize over 50 attachments! Without a doubt this machine will work out just perfect and will be the talk at the all important coffee shops in town, which is sure to bring me in more business."

How your attitude can effect your ability to collect payment.

There are so many reasons why starting your lawn care business can be tough. One of the reasons is how your attitude can effect your ability to collect payments from customers. When a person has a normal job, they should have a normal attitude, but many times an employee can go about their work and never interact with the customer. They may interact with other office staff and their attitude can effect how well things operate in that office, but it most likely doesn't effect them getting their regular paycheck.

As an entrepreneur, you become an actor on a stage that is watched by your customers and the public. If you are friendly, you will find a lot more success than if you have a chip on your shoulder or get easily frustrated. Running a business, especially early on, can present you with many situations that frustrate you but as you will see, your attitude will effect your ability to get paid.

One member of the Gopher Lawn Care Business Forum wrote "I am done with chasing customers! I have five customers that still haven't paid me for this month's lawn care. I've chased them every day so far & now I'm just gonna say f-it.

I wish they at least had the balls to call me & just say, 'well the grass isn't growing, & I'd like to cancel your services. Do they do this? Noooo! They would rather avoid & burn their bridges with me. This gets on my last nerve. Five customers are lost. I wish there was some way I could get their lawns to grow like crazy, so they could call me & I could tell them SORRY NOT INTERESTED!

None of them will be accepted for my service next year unless I get every penny up front. I'm going to write up a letter for next year that says the following so I don't have to put up with this anymore.

    * Miss a payment for 1 week, service is stopped.
    * Miss a payment for 2 weeks, service is canceled & I will add a late fee.
    * Miss a payment for 3 weeks, service is permanently canceled.

I need some sort of way to make sure I get my money. Getting paid is brutal."

One lawn care business owner suggested "I am sorry to hear you have such a hard time getting paid. One reason you might be having such troubles is due to the way you invoice and accept payment. Another reason might be your attitude. The way I invoice, I have never have an issue accepting checks. All my customers pay me on time, or early. I never have to ask twice, and some pay me up to 2 weeks early. Two of them pay me a month in advance.

I'd suggest not getting so upset about this. Sometimes customers simply just forget. A friendly reminder on the phone or in the mail usually works for me. In the past, I have considered running late fees for the stragglers, but I haven't done that yet."

Another lawn care business owner said "I have never had a payment issue taking checks either. I have one customer that pays late all the time but he still pays. At one point I thought I was going to have a big problem when he got behind a couple of months, but all it took was me picking up the phone to offer a friendly reminder and BANG I got a check paying the account in full."

A third lawn care business owner shared "When I take on a new customer I explain to them why I need to be paid on time. There are several reasons that are all tied to keeping my costs down and my rates affordable.

1 - Non paying customers cause price increase for paying customers.
2 - To keep rates low, cash flow must be maintained. Non payment hinders that.
3 - Bad checks cost me money. If I can't trust you to pay on time, can I trust your check to clear? (of course this is said 'diplomatically'.)

Above all else, try and keep a friendly level of communication with your customers and you should be able to avoid any payment issues. When customers are late to pay, try to stay friendly. The minute you get angry, all bets are off. Remember, your goal is not just to get paid but to keep the customer for a long time. When you look at the potential amount of money you can make over a lifetime from one customer, you may find yourself handling things a little more diplomatically."

What should you do with your tax refund?

If you paid more taxes last year than you owed, you will be getting a refund. Sometimes it's a little and sometimes it's a lot. What should you do with this money? Is there anything you can do to help your lawn care business grow from it? That's a question a member of the Gopher Lawn Care Business Forum asked.

He wrote "I am receiving $1,380.80 in income tax return this year. What should I do with it? Here are two options I am considering.

Option 1

Get myself a lawn vacuum to speed up my crazy cleanup calls that I am currently having. The unit sells for $1,499.95 so it would almost be paid off. I could also finance this machine but I don't want another loan on myself.

or

Option 2

I would upgrade my cell phone to improve the communication of my lawn care business. Currently, my phone is with another subscriber and I would have to pay the cancellation fee since I have 1 year left which is $240. I can get a smart phone for $19.99 the phone only and $50/month for a decent plan. I would also use the rest of the income tax money to pay off credit card/bills I have.

So what should I do? I am leaning towards option #1."

One lawn care business owner suggested "if you spend it on your vacuum, you need to consider how long it would take you to recover the investment. The improved speed it gives you to perform the work should allow you to get the jobs done faster but would that be enough to justify purchasing it?

I would personally use it to reduce my debt unless I could recover the machine investment in like 1 month and then I could do #2 on the list with that extra cash."

Another lawn care business owner said "I win a lot of business by having a smart phone. All my emails come to it and I respond right away. I email pictures to clients of my current job progress which they may then show to others, which has brought in business. So in short it pays for itself.

Based on the time of the year, I probably would not invest in a leaf collector now. If you want to speed things up buy a sweeper for around $350.00 and if you decide to sell it, you will get $250+ +. It will pay for itself very quick if you already have a tractor to pull it with. Use the rest of the cash as working capital or what other services could you offer that you could invest in.

I like the idea of paying off debt especially when the interest level is high. But the downside is that unless you can keep to a budget, you will quickly increase that credit card debt right back up again and all that money will be gone.

Buying equipment tends to be a crap shoot at times if it's not something you are going to be using daily.

Instead, why not bank as much of that money as possible. Get into the habit of saving money. Get used to having money in your bank account. Rent any equipment as needed and schedule similar jobs that need such equipment close together so you can get a bunch done as quickly as possible.

If a new cell phone with added features will help improve your communication and land you more customers, go with that too."

MARKETING

Lawn truck signs can make a big difference!

Looking like a lawn care business versus looking like someone towing a trailer full of lawn equipment can make a big difference when it comes to success. If you are operating a lawn care business and sitting there scratching your head, trying to figure out why you aren't as busy as you want to be, consider this example. A new lawn care business owner wrote us on the Gopher Lawn Care Business Forum and shared with us a picture of his lawn truck and trailer setup.

He wrote "here is my lawn care equipment setup! This is my first year in business and hopefully the first of many more to come"

The picture he included showed a nondescript pickup truck with a bland trailer behind it. Now if you, as a home owner, were driving by this set up, would you be able to tell if this was a commercial lawn care operation or a private person transporting his lawn care equipment?

It's easy to look at another business and be critical of it without reflecting on ourselves. But this does get you thinking. How does your lawn care truck and trailer compare to this one? Does yours scream out looking for attention? Do you have signs on your truck and trailer? What about a business card dispenser? If you don't have any of this, what are you waiting for! This is a small step that can bring you many new customers.

Another lawn care business owner shared with us how important lawn care trailer signs are when he wrote "signage makes a big difference and has brought me many jobs. Just the other day a customer even saw my truck at the post office and called me from the parking lot. I came out and we talked. It ended up being a very big project which should be finished tomorrow.

I've had plenty of people ask for lawn care estimates and then when I show up with all my signs and equipment, they mention, 'oh I've seen you around the area quite a bit, you must be busy!'

A small investment in signs can make a big difference in your presentation."

Now imagine if you pull up to give an lawn care estimate with signs on your truck and trailer, right after another lawn care business owner leaves with no signs. Your presentation will show the potential customer you are not a fly by night operation and they can trust you will be professional and get the job done. Having truck and trailer signs can help seal the deal with a new customer before you even start to speak.

So remember to take full advantage of all that advertising space on your lawn care truck and trailer and get your signs made today!

Spring lawn care marketing letter.

When you are trying to come up with a spring lawn care marketing letter, a member of the Gopher Lawn Care Business Forum had some great points on topics you should consider. He suggested in your letter you should

    1. send letters to last year clients, with letterhead
    2. mention organic fertilization
    3. go for exciting, energetic wording
    4. ask for referrals, recommendations, suggestions
    5. suggest now be a good time to refresh ground cover
    6. remind clients of schedule, season start, and how regular maintenance will be managed
    7. keep communication open and invite feedback

Here is a sample spring lawn care letter you can edit and use to fit your needs. Remember to try and hit some of the above mentioned key points and you should find some positive responses from those you reach out to.

Dear customer,

First things first, Happy New Year! Last year was a challenging year and now that this new year is here, we're excited about all the new changes and opportunities the new year brings!

February is the perfect time to condition the soil for the growing season. One great new opportunity is the addition of organic fertilization application to the services we offer. It's called Gluten-8, and the advantages it has vastly outweigh those of conventional chemical fertilization. Gluten-8 works twofold in that it promotes a healthy, nutrient rich environment that enables the turf to thrive, as well as being an all natural pre-emergent against weeds.

Now is also a great time for core aeration of the lawn. Core aeration helps to increase water intake, reduce water runoff and puddling, stimulate root development, reduce soil compaction, increase the tolerance to heat and drought stress, improve resiliency and cushioning, and enhance thatch breakdown.

We would also like to remind everyone of our spring clean-up services, and now would be a good time to get the overgrowth cleared out behind your garage, beside the shed, around the hedges, or at the brush-line of your property. We've found that even though most weeds still grow during the dormant season, many weeds don't and even those that are still alive are at their weakest point during this time of year. This makes for a really good time to get rid of them.

Sincerely,

Your Name

Tips to improve your lawn care business website.

There are many small steps you can take to improve your lawn care business website. Here are just a few that were discussed on the Gopher Lawn Care Business Forum.

One lawn care business owner talked about what he did to improve his website and increase the amount of people who visited it. He wrote "I have recently started writing articles on my lawn care blog. They are all of my own content. I spend some of my off time researching for the articles and putting them together. Others are simply discussions on jobs I have done.

Another small tweak that has made a big difference is adding before and after pictures. They really generate interest. I noticed this especially with pressure washing. I can't believe how many people commented on our images and said if you can do that to my deck/siding, we need to talk."

We have talked about writing articles in the past but how important do you really think they are? Are they more important to get search engines to direct to you or will potential customers read them?

"I think getting the right key words in the articles is critical. I have close to 12,000 hits last month with little advertising. My website has generated significant revenue. I down loaded a program that assists me in choosing keywords. Once installed, the program asks me for links to my competitors websites to find what keywords they are using. I then included those keywords on various pages, submitted my site to all the engines and within 30 days I had over taken every competing lawn care business search engine ranking, in our city.

It's important to remember, people like pictures. I have found that pictures on my website or pages containing them are the most visited. While I did start a blog, it doesn't seem to attract as much activity as pages with pictures. People, in my experience, want you to come look and tell them what to do. Having pictures on your website inspires them and gets them to call you."

Think that 1-800 marketing service is a good deal? Think again.

Have you looked around and seen other lawn care businesses that use those vanity numbers like 1-800-lawn-mowing? Most all of them have signed up with a company that has secured a few memorable 1-800 numbers and for a fee will forwards calls that come from a certain zip code, to your phone. You may think having a memorable 1-800 number would lead to more calls, but for at least one lawn care business owner who experimented with such a service, he found that not to be the case. Here is his story that he shared with us on the Gopher Lawn Care Business Forum.

He wrote "I just want to let other lawn care business owners know that they need to be careful when they enter into a contract with a marketing company. Read your contract carefully and do not enter into any contract unless you understand your obligations, the marketing company's obligation, and exactly what your expectations are about the results from that company. Also, make sure that their ideas match the business ethics you have set for your company. That will not necessarily come out in the initial consultation. If you are not careful at the beginning, you will find yourself spending a bunch of money with no recourse to stop the bleeding.

We chose to sign up with a company that secured the vanity number 1-800-###-#### because that is what they had available. WE WERE WRONG! The vanity # you choose should match the company and it's personality. You should not have to revamp your entire marketing strategy to fit the vanity #. We are a lawn care company. We were very excited in the beginning and we spent gobs of money putting the vanity # on everything. Trucks, mailers, signs, invoices, statements, webpage and web advertising, even radio advertising. It was not long that we noticed that the only calls we were getting on the vanity # were our customers with billing or service questions.

It stands to reason, if you advertise a phone #, people will call it. People call whatever number is most convenient. Because that was the number on invoices and statements that was the number they would call. We also found out that new customers were not getting the number off of the trucks. Rather, they were approaching the technicians and getting a business card to call, because they wanted to meet and interview, even if just for a moment, the person doing the work.

In my opinion, you can advertise any number and you will get the phone to ring.

There is a lot more to this story, but the bottom line is, this marketing did not work for us, and when we approached the company about our concerns, their approach was to try to prove that the system was working with no offer to help us adjust the strategy to make it work for us. Just be careful what you do and make sure you know the people you are dealing with."

Another lawn care business owner said "I had a meeting with the similar company a few months ago. We had a great talk, but in the long run I could not come to grips with paying $200 a month for a phone number. They had a great sales pitch. By the time you finish talking with the rep you felt like running for your check book. But I had to stop and think. I said to myself, why pay them when I can do the same thing for pennies on the dollar. That's why I chose to get my own 1-800 number which now costs me under $10 per month."

In the end, you have to keep in mind that you are promoting their 1-800 number. You are helping them build value in their phone number. Over time they can raise your price and you will have no recourse but to cancel service. If you stop paying, they can resell the number to a competitor in your area. Why bother with a high priced vanity number when in the big picture, no one cares about a phone number. You can purchase your own toll free number for much cheaper.

Economic bail out plan lawn care marketing campaign.

Are you trying to make your lawn care marketing stand out from your competitors? I am sure you are. A great way to come up with new marketing ideas is to pay attention to current events. One lawn care business owner on the Gopher Lawn Care Business Forum shared with us his new idea of creating a lawn care marketing campaign that played off of the economic stimulus packages.

He wrote "I was thinking about doing some marketing that came across as I was helping the economy. Offering a special deal to the first 25-50 customers. The deal would be billed as an economic bail out plan of like $35 a cut when you sign an annual lawn care contract for a year. The lot size must be under a 1/2 acre. What do you think. Would this be a good idea to experiment with?

I think I'm going to put it in the newspapers and also the senior centers newspapers. As for a heading I think if I put 'Economic Bail Out Plan' everyone will want to look at it."

Another lawn care business owner shared "almost all of my advertisement this year is going to have an economic twist to it. When you put together a piece of marketing material you have to remember to include a closing line in it, otherwise it becomes just another boring flier or postcard from a lawn care company. You need to make it zing. You want your ad to make people say yes that weren't even considering lawn care before seeing your ad!

Also don't waste money on an expensive ad in the newspaper! Buy a little one liner in the classified section that says quality lawn care with your web address and phone number . . I have one that cost me $15 a month and says

Quality lawn care
www.yourwebaddress.com
888-555-9237

You also may want to consider spending your money on joining your local Chamber of Commerce and BBB. I have found that will bring in far more calls than a news paper ad."

We fix cheap lawn care cuts.

Marketing should always be about promoting what you have and what others don't. It should accentuate your positives and eliminate your negatives. We talk about this concept often on the Gopher Lawn Care Business Forum and here is a great real world example of it being implemented.

A lawn care business owner wrote "In my area there are easily more than 100 lawn care companies. Many of the bigger lawn care companies are offering lawn mowing starting as low as $12 a cut even though the cost should be much higher. By offering lawn care so cheaply they are making it harder for the rest of us to survive. Most of these businesses hire undocumented workers whom they pay dirt cheap wages and throw them on a bunch of zero turn mowers.

I refuse to advertise based on price, I would much rather promote our quality of work. In an effort to separate my lawn care company from the rest of the pack I am designing a flyer based around the fact that we don't use big riding mowers on your home.

I can show my customers the lawns that have been cut with the big zero turn mowers and they can see the difference. Besides they compact soil and leave tire marks, they also seem to leave too much uneven and scalped grass. For most residential yards a walk-behind is plenty of mower."

That is a real fantastic marketing angle. If your competitors use big lawn mowers that they race across the lawns with, why not use the marketing angle that you use smaller mowers and offer a higher quality cut. This is brilliant.

I also like that you are using a big eye catching graphic of the mower with the red bar across it and the title 'We Fix Cheap Lawn Cuts' on your flyer. It really grabs your attention and gets your message across.

How will you be distributing your lawn care flyer?

"I got 10,000 flyers printed up and I will be using a canvassing company to distribute them to local homes. I pay the company $.08 per flyer. One person on average can pass out 100 flyers per hour. Paying the $.08 per flyer is about the same as paying an employee $8 an hour. If you factor in your time supervising you actually save money going with a company. The company I work with can do 20,000 in one day. Just make sure you go with a reliable company (ASK FOR REFERENCES !!!) I've seen guys get burned by not doing their homework. If you choose a poorly run company they can just take your money and toss the flyers in the garbage, so be aware of this."

Park bench lawn care marketing idea.

There are an infinite number of ways to get your lawn care marketing message out to potential lawn care customers and the Gopher Lawn Care Business Forum is chock full of them. When you are considering implementing a new marketing idea you have to make sure you are getting your message out to the proper demographic group. For lawn care, a good group is a homeowner with disposable income that wants their weekends free to relax. What better place to find such potential customers than at a golf course! That is exactly what this business owner did.

He wrote "I came up with a marketing idea last weekend while playing golf. I was sitting on the bench at Hole 9 and was thinking how crappy the bench was. I thought to myself, if I built a bench for the golf course holes, the club owner would probably love it. He'd be getting new benches Free and I could get my marketing message out!

So after playing I talked to the club owner and told him that I would make two new benches for him on hole 1 and 10 as long as I could put my advertising on the back. He said yes and asked if I would do all the holes. I told him that I would get people for the other holes.

I looked around and found the parts to put the benches together. It cost me $160 for each bench and the best part was the club owner actually gave me $200 back because he just loves his new benches. That only cost me $120 for both benches and they stay there for as long as I want. I am sure they could be made for even cheaper if you are handy with wood.

I put the bench next to the hole yardage and put my outdoor business card holders on the pole next to the bench. People look at the ad and take a card.

But my story is not done yet! Now that I was invigorated from my success, I talked to the local gas station owners that I deal with and they all said it would be okay to put my bench outside around the stores. There is always great spots next to the air or vacuum machines.

It's free advertising for me and all I have to do is build the bench!"

Can you tell us a little about the specifics of the bench? What did you do to actually construct it and get your message on it?

"My friend owns a fence company, so I used vinyl fence for the back and seat of the bench. Then I had a full color sticker printed to put on the back."

Lawn care business flyer discussion.

What do you do when you can't find the exact lawn care flyer template you want to represent your lawn care business? You make your own up from scratch of course! That is what a member of the Gopher Lawn Care Business Forum did when he shared with us a little about his new lawn care marketing campaign.

He wrote "here is my lawn care flyer that I designed myself. Believe it or not I did it using a regular word processor. So for those who think they can't put together a flyer that stands out unless you have some high dollar graphic program, think again. The only thing I paid for was to have it printed. It cost me around $150 and they also corrected any grammar issues they found for free. I have been getting a bunch of calls from it now so I know it is working.

Besides going door to door, another way I will be distributing my flyers is through a local pizzeria. I will be getting together with my local pizza places to attach them to the boxes.

Where did I find the inspiration for the design? Well I figured I wanted to make this flyer stand out. I looked at a handful of competitor's flyers and I just wasn't impressed with them. I feel this one is a definite eye grabber. To give a few pointers to others who are wanting to make their own flyers, remember to use a lot of color. You want to be able to stand out from every one else. Also don't be afraid to use a lot of text. Many times, if a potential customer doesn't see a service they need, they will throw your flyer away. Finally, make some kind of offer to get the potential customer to call by offering some sort of discount or sale.

My lawn care flyer says:

If you have property and want it maintained to it's utmost beauty,

we are the company you are looking for. That's our promise…
Walkways • Patios • Full Lawn Care • Landscape Design &
Installation

Here are a few services we provide
FREE Estimates
Edging,
Sod installation, Curbing,
Landscape Design/Install, Driveway Sealing
Stump grinding, Pavers
Minor irrigation repair, Walkways/driveways
Landscape renovation, General Cleanup
New lawn installation, Gutter/Roof Cleanup
Over seeding, Low risk Tree Removal
Aeration, Mulching
Color Installation, Snow removal/Ice Control
And much much more……

A little about us:
We strive for customer satisfaction. If you are tired of the hassle
of fly-by-night lawn maintenance companies that are here today,
gone tomorrow, if you are having difficulties with your present
lawn care provider, please give us the opportunity to properly
maintain your lawn to its fullest potential.

Some of the little things we strive to provide our customers with:

   * All employees are dressed in uniform.
   * We leave all gates the way we found them
   * We blow all debris and dust caused by our service off hard
surfaces driveways, patios and walks.
   * We blow all grass clippings and debris out of flower beds.
   * We don't allow grass to clump from damp weather
conditions, we vacuum all clippings.
   * We don't allow any weeds in beds, as long as beds have an
adequate amount of mulch.

Customers we accept:
We accept all customer's. No job is too big or too small. We provide services to residential, commercial, and industrial. And we care about everyone."

Lawn care marketing success is found in quality not quantity.

Most new lawn care businesses start out with a lot of time on their hands and little money. You may think this puts you at a disadvantage, but that is not the case. It actually is the exact ingredients you need to find success in your lawn care marketing. As you will see in this discussion, the key to success in lawn care marketing is found in the quality of your campaign, not in the quantity. A new business owner brought this up in the Gopher Lawn Care Business Forum.

He wrote "I started my lawn care business as a part time extra income deal. I really enjoy it and want to expand it to be my full time income. I didn't start until late June and currently have only 7 customers. I feel I will need to get to approximately 50 customers to achieve the income I need. I have already obtained my business license and am in the process of getting insurance. I really need some advice on when would be a good time to start marketing to residential customers. I don't have much money to spend on it and I feel like my timing is very important. If I am too early, will my flyers be misplaced or if I am too late, will they get thrown out? Any advice would be helpful."

One lawn care business owner said, "in my opinion, there are two ways to do this, either you go for pinpoint shots or you go for shotgun blast marketing. If you are going for shotgun blast marketing, you have to expect it to bring lower returns for more money. You will have to figure out your budget and if you only have the money to do one round of fliers or door hangers, you should distribute them right before the season starts in your area. If you got enough to hit them more like 2-3 times then I would start a month before the season then do it every 30 days. You'll need a min of 5,000 fliers if you get a 1% return and then it's up to you to close the deal. I would say you need 10-20,000 flyers if you want to do more than one round.

Around here it will take you about 20 seconds per house to hang door hangers. So 3 houses a minute. That's 180 an hr. Or 1440 in a 8hr day. Do that for 3 days and you knocked out 4320 hangers. At 1% that's 43 call backs. 2% would be 86 call backs. 43 + 7= 50.

If you are going for pinpoint marketing accuracy, you will need to spend time talking to people, but also less money. Personally, I like the idea of anything where you are making person contact with your potential clients. That does more than one thing. First, it lets you leave a good first impression. Second, if they let you give an estimate, you can do a better follow up and in one way or another, possibly get the sale with your contact right there.

For me personally, if you mail me something, or hang something on my door, I will probably file it with all the rest of the junk mail. If I can connect a face and a name to it, have a need for what they are selling, and if I like the person, I am far more likely to hang on to their material than if I get it in the mail, etc. I am also far more likely to use them on the spot. I tend to reward a good sales person, if it is done right and in good taste (if I have a need for the product or service).

One thing I would like to mention about placing anything on a garage door is that I have noticed a LOT of people open their garage door when they pull onto the street or when they are like a block away. Now I know that is a terrible idea, safety and security wise, but people do it so their door is open when they get there and are ready to drive in. Now lets think what if going to happen to that magnet or flier if it is stuck on their garage door. The door is going to be all the way open before they even get close enough to see that anything was on the door. Just a thought....

So with all that said, consider going out in the evenings (or Saturdays) and knocking on doors for a couple hours. When I have a slow day, I will do this all day long. I find that after about 6pm or so people tend to be home. There are down sides to this as well but in my opinion, this is the best time to do it if you want to make contact with the person and probably going to be the time when you get the best results as well. Something that I would caution you on is, when it starts getting dark outside, STOP KNOCKING ON DOORS! When people can not see you without turning on the porch light, they do not want to have you knocking on their door. Especially not to sell a lawn mowing service. Besides, at this point you would not be able to get a good look at the yard anymore to give them a good estimate."

How a lawn care business should write a classified ad.

We got into a discussion about classified ads on the Gopher Lawn Care Business Forum. This is a very important topic because a lot of lawn care business owners experiment with them. Print media is not yet dead. As long as your potential customers are reading the newspaper everyday, classified advertising is still a viable marketing method to attract them. No matter what marketing method you are using, you always want to get the most bang for your buck. Here are some tips on how to make your classified ads as effective as possible.

Here are three quick basic rules you need to follow:

1. The top line of your classified ad is your headline. It MUST be something that freezes a readers eyes in their tracks and stops them from continuing on in their scanning of the page. If you fail to do this, you have lost any chance you had at them reading further.
2. The next few lines of your ad are your body. The text found in there must keep the excitement going and build up the momentum to get the reader ready to act.
3. End with a call to action. Tell the reader what they should do to get the great offer you just made.

With those rules in mind, let's now jump to a classified ad that fails this test.

ABC LAWNCARE
888-555-5555
all calls returned
spring special 20% off first month of new lawn service
services available: mowing, edging, mulching, powerwashing

storm clean up

First off, using your business name in the headline WILL NOT GRAB THE READERS ATTENTION. It absolutely fails rule #1. Business owners do this all the time because they are so proud of their ad. They are proud of their business name too. They want to show the world how proud they are. This is a huge reason why such ads fail.

Second line is the phone number. As I read it I have to ask myself, why would I call this business? Let me look to the third line which says 'all calls returned.' Well I certainly hope all calls that come into that business are returned. That is not enough for me. Most readers would pass right by this ad.

Now on the opposite end of the spectrum is the classified ad that reads:

FREE LAWN MOWING
I will mow your lawn for free.
Find out how! Call now!!
xxx-xxx-xxxx

Free always seems to be the key word in advertising that stops a reader dead in their tracks. If you ran an ad like this, you would most certainly get more calls than the one above. With this ad you could have a promotion where if a lawn care customer signed up with you for an annual contract, they could get 1 or 2 free mowings throughout the year.

The customer would benefit because they would be getting something they could use for free. You would benefit because you would get a lawn care customer that would generate revenue all year long.

The more outrageous the offer, the more response you will get.

Sure instead of free mowing, you could say, free estimates. But won't the reader know that everyone gives free estimates? Put yourself in the consumers position for a moment when you think about this. Which offer would get you motivated to call? If one stands out over the other, use it!

You will also want to experiment with the ad's position. Some newspapers allow you to pay for a higher ranking ad. If you can afford to go with the first spot, go for it. Also experiment with using the business services section of the classified ads, over the services offered section. It seems when newspaper readers are looking for contractors, they look in the business section first. The reason is readers feel these advertisers will be legitimate vs. someone simply working out of their trunk.

As with all your marketing efforts, test them. Try something, track the results and then change one element of your ad to see if it increases the response rate. If it does, experiment again by changing one more element. Keep this experimentation cycle going and you will find much growth in your future.

7 Tips to improve your lawn care website's search engine ranking.

Does your lawn care business have a website? If you do, congratulations you are ahead of the game. Many new lawn care business owners put off a website for far too long. It's important to have a website to attract lawn care customers that are searching the internet for local lawn care providers. But just having a website is not enough. If a potential customer can't find your site, they won't be calling you. Instead they will be calling your competitor.

Don't fret when it comes to improving the search engine ranking of your website. There are a few simple steps you can take to get your website to rank higher than it is now. The best part about these tips is they are easy to implement and you can use them right now.

A web designer shared with us his tips and tricks on the Gopher Lawn Care Business Forum. He wrote "here are a few pointers to help promote your site and business.

1. Build links from as many related sites as possible to your site.
2. Make sure to always include a unique Title & Description for every page.
3. Include your most important keywords in the title and description.
4. Focus, don't try to cover more than 1 or 2 topics on a page.
5. Every page should have an h1 tag.
6. Don't use Flash for constructing your site, it's Ok to include some flash content, but remember search engines can't read flash.
7. Never ever try to fool the search engines. No hiding white text on white background or other deceptive practices."

If you are looking for still more ways to improve your search engine rankings, why not make some short video commercials that promote your service and upload them to sites like youtube.com. In the video description, include your keywords, company name, contact information, and web address. Having back links from popular sites like the many video hosting sites, can really help. If you don't have the ability to make a video commercial, what about a slide show that is saved into a video file format?

Do a search for your website's keywords like (your town & lawn care). Then make a note of how far down in the search results you find your website link. Afterward, start to implement some of these search engine optimization tips and track your search engine results after a few months. You may be pleasantly surprised to see your rank has improved!"

Going big come hell or high water with my lawn care marketing.

You'd be amazed how much business you could drum up if you put your mind to it. Most lawn care business owners tend to spend more time working on jobs than marketing. What if you stepped up your marketing effort a little more? If you did, where would you put that additional energy? Would you hand out a few more business cards? Maybe distribute a few more lawn care flyers?

A member of the Gopher Lawn Care Business Forum shared with us his aggressive lawn care marketing plan. You may want to compare your plan with his and see where you could improve. He wrote "this year I decided to go big, come hell or high water. I started aggressively marketing residential and commercial. Because of the new contacts I made, I just recently had the opportunity to bid on 5 large apartments. These jobs will be very good money and could launch me into the six figure income range. I will hopefully be signing the contracts next week.

I am keeping all of my residential customers as I grow my commercial side. I will definitely have to hire some more help this year. I will also have to buy more equipment. I have found the key to success in the lawn care business is similar to any other industry. You have to aggressively market your business and strive to do the best job possible.

As far as marketing I do it all. I use lawn signs in locations that I want to drum up more work. I run newspaper ads in the local paper. I visit all real estate companies. I also drive around town and look for more customers. I stop at apartments, doctors offices, truck stops etc… I will stop and ask for business wherever I can. I hand out cards to everyone I meet and give cards to all my friends and family to hand out.

I have found it to be very important to market to my existing customer base. This type of marketing is different because they know you and trust you. I try to sell them on other services they could use. For example I offer weeding of the flower beds, trimming low hanging trees, pressure washing, and gutter cleaning. I even cleaned a backyard pond and painted shutters. These are all services that I look for when I am on a job.

I always go the extra mile to help my customers and make their yards the best in the neighborhood. This helps me to go to them and ask them to help me find more work. They recommend me every chance they can. I ask them to refer me to their friends and family, even if they do have a lawn service at the time. I find that if they can get me in contact to offer a free quote I can work my magic and find more work. Once the door is open I have the opportunity to sell. Most people would love to have someone cut their grass but think it is too expensive. I show them that it is not too expensive and that their yard can look a lot better. For every new contract that I sign from them, I give them a $25.00 gift card. I also advertise that I take all credit cards as payment. This is a very good selling point for a lot of customers.

Much of my new business comes from the phone book and newspaper ads. This is also the most costly form of advertizing that I do. Again one or two annual contracts pays this for the entire year.

In addition I became a member of an internet contractor referral service group. They do the advertising and when a job comes up in my area they send me the contact. I in turn pay them between $5 and $18 dollars for the contact. This has worked out extremely well. I have not changed my cost at all when using this service. I bid against other locally approved companies. I don't get every one, but with the cost of the leads being so low, I can quickly make up those costs. One annual contract more than pays for the full years worth of leads that I get from them.

I am not shy about my business. I tell everyone about it and I ask for the work and you should too!"

When is the right time to get lawn care customers?

What a great discussion this is. Trying to figure out when is the right time to get lawn care customers. If you are new to the lawn care business or you haven't started yet, you could potentially be picking different times of the year when you think it would be the best. You might even hold off your marketing until that time, but as we will see in this discussion, you would be making a big mistake. Let's look at this discussion from the Gopher Lawn Care Business Forum and see what we can learn from it.

A new lawn care business owner wrote "when is the right time to get lawn care customers? I am planning to open up a landscaping company and want to know the best time to attract customers.

Spring seems to be ideal because that is when people think about lawn care, BUT, the customers that get yearly service usually sign a seasonal contract over the winter, which leaves no room for me to convince them to switch.

Next I was thinking possibly at the end of the summer. I can go door by door, talk to the homeowner and sell my services in advance so that they remember me for the following year and they don't sign the contract with the other lawn care company. The following spring I could then go back to them and have them sign one of my lawn care contracts.

Now, I know that they might forget about me from August all the way to spring time and might end up signing a contract anyway with the other company. So I was thinking, what if I write down the potential customer's address. I could then send them a Christmas card in the winter which would remind them that I'm still around and that I still consider them a future potential customer. The card would also help me because they would see I took the time to send them a Christmas card.

Do you think this is a good approach? Anything I can add to this idea"

First off, you can tell this marketing plan is WAAAAAAAAAAAAAY over thought. It is way too busy and too complex and needs to scraped. Other lawn care business owners agreed and offered advice on what should be done.

One wrote "the best time to attract lawn care customers is every chance you get! Any time you get 5 or 10 extra minutes, walk up to 5 houses and introduce yourself. Do this a few times and you will start getting calls."

A second said "I feel it is always the right time to land new clients. Every time you service a new customer you should ALWAYS 'Clover Leaf' the immediate homes around it with fliers, introducing your company.

Clover Leafing means you hang door hangers or flyers at neighbors of your customer. The flyers should say something like 'TAKE A LOOK AT YOUR NEIGHBORS, THEY USE OUR SERVICES. GIVE US A CALL WE PROVIDE FREE ESTIMATES. Then list a few services you provide. CLOVER LEAFING WORKS! Hang 2 or 3 houses on both sides, do this across the street and behind the house. Most people try to keep up with the 'Jones' as they say and it is true most do. When you provide great service, word of month advertising will kick in.

Clover Leafing works for me, it has worked for 25 years, and will continue to work! You NEVER put anything IN the mail box, instead you HANG it ON the mail box or door.

We had a goal to increase our client base by 20 to 25% this year and it was surpassed by that much before the season even started! So I know it works. Experiment with changing the ad on your flyers. There are many different ways to do it but you will find there is only a few ways to do it right, that makes it effective. Only through experimentation will you find this out.

The bottom line is, anytime is the right time to market and bring on new customers. Along with any new customer you service you should be trying to market this service to the homes around it as well.

Look at it like this, if you leave out one house or one neighbor that means you have left out one potential customer even if that customer was a one time customer. Isn't it nice to have several customers on one street so you don't have to drive and waste time and fuel going from one customer to the next?

We service 4 major upper class communities and on one street we have five customers out of 8 homes, so we can park the truck in one place and service all of them from there. This saves me a lot of money.

If you are looking for commercial clients, depending on their budget setting time frame, send a request letter to be placed on their bidders list. Most commercial facilities set budgets in Jan, July, or Oct. and they will contact you when their property is up for bid. It also doesn't hurt you to follow up with them to make sure they do."

I just started and can't get any lawn care customers. Why?

There is no doubt the toughest time in your business life will be the start up phase. That is when you have to learn how to go from a dead stop to a run before you run out of start up cash. But what can a business owner do to attract new customers? It can be so frustrating. Especially when you see competitor's ads that promote a lawn mowing price cheaper than you can offer it. As crazy as things may seem when you are frantically looking for customers, there are ways to find them. This is a topic brought up to us on the Gopher Lawn Care Business Forum by a new member.

She wrote "my husband and I have started a lawn care business. We have invested a little money, about $1,000.00 so far. We have the business license, getting a DBA with our next customer check, working on getting insurance, literally waiting on a quote right now. We have signs on the truck, business cards, website and professional looking quote sheets and invoices. I go out and look for work, while my husband and son work the yards. We just recently landed some work with a realty company. I did a quote on a commercial property today and am keeping my fingers crossed that we get it. We also had just landed a seasonal contact with a residential customer too.

The problem we are having is actually getting the jobs. I am pushing the professional part of it, we do great work. Our web site has before and after pics of some of the properties we have worked on. I know it's just going to take time, but we have an over abundance of competition in our area, since the economy is so bad right now. It seems like everyone has a mower and a truck. I am trying to make my company stand out from the rest.

I guess what I am asking is, does any one have any ideas on how we can get the business so we can show a profit. We have thought about the off season and have ideas on what to offer our yearly customers like leaf removal, storm clean up and various other non lawn related items. How we can make it better though? We really need to make some money to pay the bills. It's just so hard to start up when you have people out there doing lawns for $15-20 dollars. It seems everyone wants that type of price."

Lawn care companies depend on relationships with their customers. How should you go about building relationships? One simple step you can take is to make your 'about us' website page a bit more personal. Take a few pictures of your equipment. This lets customers know the type of equipment you use. Include some photos of your husband & yourself too. This helps the customer to see a familiar face when you come to do an estimate on their lawn. Being comfortable helps set the stage for a sale.

Keep knocking on doors and telling everyone you meet about your business. Sales all start with human interactions. The average person won't care if a company has a website. They won't care if a company has a door hanger. They won't care if they have uniforms. All of these things can help but they are not the most important part.

The most important part is the customer knows the business owner and feels comfortable with them. Especially when it's a small business.

Think about it. You would hire a friend of yours first and every time over an unknown business when given the chance. Knowing this, it is important to go out and meet new people. Also focus on letting the people you already know, that you are now in business.

Once you get customers, ask them what other services they need done. Point out issues you see with their property and tell them how you can resolve the issues. The more problems you can solve for them the more they will call upon you for services and the more they will refer you out to their friends and family.

It's very important to work your social networks. Are you involved in any social organizations, sports or clubs in your community? Are you letting them know you are now in business? Focus on getting the word out to the people you know and then spread the message outwards. As you do this you will attract more and more quality customers.

Offering car wash incentives to get customers to sign up.

A lot of lawn care business owners have experiences and skills from others industries that may not seem to mesh with lawn care at first glance. With some creativity, they may end up meshing perfectly. Take for instance this new lawn care business owner who shared with us his story on the Gopher Lawn Care Business Forum. He used to work as an auto detailer and found mixing his skills could attract new lawn care customers.

He wrote "for many years I have been a professional auto detailer and am now getting into the lawn and landscaping business. I still do some auto detailing and I enjoy it but it is too dependent on the weather. The weather plays a large role in how often the customer will want his car detailed. When I detail a boat or auto, I call the customer back in 3 months time to schedule their next wash and wax. But their response will depend on the weather or if they have time.

When I looked around at the top detailers in the industry a lot of them are upselling wax at $50 to $60 per car. I don't want to do that as I have found it hard to find an employee who can put wax on an $80,000 Mercedes and get a swirl free job.

I would much rather sell a service, like lawn mowing once and service it over and over again. To me I enjoy the game of marketing and offering top notch customer service and sales.

One of the marketing incentives I am using now is I offer new lawn care customers a free wash and wax after their first 4 cuts. Then after six months I give them a free auto detailing. This will only apply to my first 40 annual lawn care clients and that is it. I use an annual contract for 12 months worth of yard work. Also I focus on full lawn service. Not piece meal stuff. The average lawn will cost $200/month which will include mowing, fertilization and weed control.

I would normally charge $65.00 per wash and wax. A full auto detailing would cost $140.00.

Time wise, it takes me and one helper about 1 hour on the wash and wax. For the full detail, it will take 2 hours. These services will be done in the evening and will be one time incentives.

When I do my marketing, I use a marketing company that can narrow my search to certain criteria to get leads from my ideal customers. These are the criteria I look for:

1. $60,000 income and up. The reason behind this is they have extra income.

2. 1 or no kids, because their kids aren't going to be cutting the lawn.

3. A credit rating of 670 or better, because they pay their bills.

4. A house value of $150,000-$600,000, because they have a decent size lawn in a nice neighborhood which will help attract other good customer.

5. They have lived in their house for more than 5 yrs. This shows stability.

6. Their age is 32 and up.

These are only guidelines remember LIFE IS ABOUT PERCENTAGES. IT IS ALL ABOUT THAT 1% better today than we were a week ago."

This is just one example of how an auto detailer was able to use his services to attract new lawn care customers. With a little creativity of your own, I am sure you can think of a unique incentive to offer new customers who sign up with your lawn care service.

OPERATIONS

Using the customer's water for pressure washing.

Many lawn care business owners look to offer additional services to supplement their lawn service income. One of the many services they choose to offer is pressure or power washing. If you choose to offer such a service you may be wondering where to get the water. That is what one member of the Gopher Lawn Care Business Forum was curious about when he wrote "is this alright? I want to add pressure washing to the list of service I offer, but I want to know if it's alright to use the client's water to do the job? I have a 2,750 PSI - 2.6 GPM pressure washer to get me started until I can afford more professional equipment."

A second business owner said "in my opinion it would be more professional to have your own water however, you aren't in the pressure washing business and hauling that big water tank around would be near impossible with all of your equipment. You are simply adding convenience to your customers by offering this service so they don't have to contact another company, write another check, etc. They will more than likely understand this, so using their water shouldn't be a huge deal. Obviously you can't charge quite as much as you could if you were using your own water, but I think the difference would be minimal."

A third business owner suggested "I think you should notify or ask the customer if they will permit you to use their water first.

What alternative do you have? It probably wouldn't be cost effective for you to buy a tank with water and put it on your truck/trailer. I suppose this could be done, but it would require more work/investment on your part than it may be worth. You would then have to charge more for this option.

The extra expenses would include these:

1. Your water
2. A tank to hold the water
3. A hose to get the water from the tank to your washer
4. In the cold weather you may have to drain the tank daily, depending on your local temps. This would take more time from you. You would have to fill the tank before the job, then to drain it afterward. If you don't have enough water in the tank then you would have to go back to your house or where ever to get more water.
5. Truck or trailer space to haul the tank."

A fourth lawn care business owner said "we only use our clients' water and yes it is fine. For a cleaning detergent we use one you can get from your local big box retailer and most work well. As far as water pressure goes, an average well will generally produce 4.5 GPM so you are good to go. If you use city water there should be no problem at all.

A 2,750 PSI power washing unit is excellent for vinyl siding but light for use on decks. However to get around this you can look into buying a turbo tip. They are around $80.00 and are worth their weight in gold.

As for pricing, we quote power washing jobs anywhere from $65.00 to $90.00 an hour."

To sum all this up, if you are looking to get started in offering pressure washing as an add-on service, using your client's water seems to be acceptable. Consider getting a smaller pressure washing unit to start and scale it up as the need for this service increases.

Do I need to bag the grass?

How does bagging grass clippings or leaving them on the lawn effect the lawn's health? Do most lawn care customers want their grass clippings bagged or do they not care? These are some of the issues you have to take into consideration when you are running a lawn care business and are trying to determine if you should bag your grass clippings or not.

A lawn care business owner wrote on the Gopher Lawn Care Business Forum about a specific lawn care situation he found himself needing help with. He wrote "I have a new customer who is going to hydro seed his lawn this spring. Should I bag the first cutting of new grass or should I mulch the grass? I am of the opinion that most people mulch their clippings way too much."

One lawn care business owner responded "We always mulch unless the customer complains the grass is growing too fast then we will bag. Do you know what kind of seed they are going to Hydroseed? I find around here they have a high mix of Rye grass which can be a problem as it dies off fast, this is another good reason to mulch."

Another lawn care business owner said "we never bag clippings. It costs too much and seems like just a waste. The blades that we have on our lawn mowers are special 'mulching' blades and they work good. When you take clippings off of the lawn, that is just fertilizer you will have to replace it with.

Initially, you should let the new grass grow higher then usual so it will properly establish. You want the new established grass to have a good root system. When it comes to cutting, only cut a maximum of 1/3 off of the grass. Any more than that and you will be hurting the grass. The grass will also start clumping up which takes more time to correct.

Some home owners understand letting the new grass grow higher to properly establish, and others will complain. Just keep this in mind to educate them."

A third business owner said "Because of the hydroseeding I would clean up any clippings or debris before it is sprayed. Also, the turf should be mowed fairly short in order for the slurry to make contact with the ground and not be floating on the blades of grass. The slurry generally contains a fertilizer mixture so worrying that you'll be removing 'free' fertilizer by taking the mulched grass away need not apply in this case.

If a lawn is mowed regularly (once per week) and you are not taking more than 1/3 of it's total length you should have no problem mulching. Some clients like the grass to be bagged as they don't want it tracked into the house by kids and pets, or commercial properties that want a crisp clean look.

If you are not mulching the turf I would recommend that you sell your clients on soil testing kits to make sure you are getting the right amounts of NPK (Nitrogen, Phosphorous, and Potassium) and adjust the fertilizing accordingly. This makes for a great selling feature for 'bagged' clients."

If you mulch all the time how do you control how mulch thatch is on the lawn? Do you de-thatch in the summer?

"Grass clippings do not add much at all to the thatch layer. If your lawn already has a thick layer of thatch it needs to be dealt with because it will slow the breakdown of the mulched grass.

If your lawn has a healthy layer of thatch (and yes thatch is all part of a healthy lawn) it will help break down the mulched grass."

What lawn care billing frequency works best?

There are so many different ways to bill your lawn care customers, the number of choices can make your head spin. What methods works well for some lawn care business owners may not work so well for others. There are many factors to consider when you are creating your billing frequency.

That is what a lawn care business owner was concerned about when he wrote on the Gopher Lawn Care Business Forum and asked "I have a question regarding billing customers. This is the beginning of my second season and I have picked up my first new customer of the year. I asked and she shared with me the reason why she left her old grass service. Last August she got billed 4 times during the month even though she only got her grass cut twice. I have heard that some older people get charged 32 weeks a year regardless if their lawn gets cuts or not. I only charge if I mow. If it is too dry then I don't cut and don't charge them.

What is the industry standard? Do you charge on a per year basis? I just charge per cut and feel that's fair. Otherwise I think there is a psychological issue the customers have to handle and that is they think at times they are getting billed for work that didn't happen. What do you guys think?"

One lawn care business owner shared "I have both per cut & annual customers who are billed monthly. With the annual customers, I multiply the number of cuts typically performed during the year to service the customer's particular turf type by the mowing fee. Then I divide that figure by 12 to get a price I will charge per month. The customer will then pay the same amount each month, year round. Heavy rains or a longer season means more cuts with no change in rate for them. A light year means less cuts to be done, still at the same rate. It's calculated on an 'average year.' If you are new, it may take you a little while to get these numbers accurate for your area."

A second lawn care business owner said "I usually charge per cut. If I don't cut due to weather then I don't charge. I think that's the best way to handle it. I usually go around once a week to cut. I mark down on a spread sheet when I mow, then I give out invoices at the end of the month."

A third business owner said "I mostly charge per month. I just explain to the customer that I may work a little less through the winter, but it evens out when I am mowing their lawn in the summer and it is 115 degrees out. They understand that I have bills to pay all year. Most people are ok with it, but you MUST explain it to them in the beginning how you will be billing them."

As you can see, there is no lawn care industry standard concerning billing methods that I have seen. Each business owner does things their own way. One thing that holds true no matter how you bill is this. It's always better to get paid in advance for your work than it is to wait for the customer to get around to pay you. So keep that in mind when you are crafting your lawn care businesses billing frequency.

How to charge bi-weekly lawn care customers.

Every lawn care customer is different and each will have a different view on how well they want their lawn maintained. Some customers will want their lawn to look as nice as possible and require a weekly mowing while others will want a cheaper job and have the lawn cut every two weeks. How should these different customers be charged though? Should there be a difference in price between weekly and bi-weekly customers? That is what a lawn care business owner was curious to see how other business owners handle this situation when he asked his question on the Gopher Lawn Care Business Forum.

He wrote "there always seems to be a lawn care customer that wants to be cheap and let his lawn overgrow for two weeks during the growing season. Should I bill the customer my regular price for mowing but instead of weekly, only bill him twice a month? I asked a friend who is also in the business and he suggested to cut the lawn very low so it's not such a pain on the return trips. He said the bi-weekly folks are great. They don't want manicured lawns. You can just get in, cut it low and get out. I am not so sure about that advice as I want to continue providing a high quality service even to my bi-weekly customers."

One lawn care business owner suggested "if you are going to mow a lawn bi-weekly in the summer, you need to charge more for it. I charge it as a cut & a half. So if a lawn is $30 weekly, it then becomes $45 bi-weekly. I have found it takes nearly twice as long to mow the lawn because it has grown a lot more since the last time I was there. It requires more gas and it's harder on the belts & blades too. If you allow a lawn care customer to save nearly 50% on lawn care expenses by switching to bi-weekly cuts, they will never shift over to weekly & have it done right.

There is a reason most lawn care business owners won't do this (actually several).

1) You can't make any money doing lawns bi-weekly.
2) These are usually the same customers that don't pay or are very slow to pay.
3) It's abusing the equipment, even though most of us run commercial gear that can take it, it will last longer if you don't abuse it.
4) The lawn will never bring you any referrals because they look bad almost all the time. By the time you get there, after 2 weeks it looks like hell. Then there's hay left when you are done so it looks crappy after too. Or you spend extra time, every time to keep cleaning it up.

Charge a cut & a half. It will cover the added expenses & they might then figure for the lousy 25% they save by going bi-weekly, they'd rather have the place look good & ask you to do it weekly.

Along the same lines…. when I get a call for an overgrown lawn I bid it pretty high.

Example: If the lawn looks like I would normally charge say $25 & it appears to have 2 months worth of summer growth on it, that's approx 8 weeks that they should have spent $25 per week = $200 so $125-$150 to knock it back down is not unreasonable. These lawns beat up your equipment, wear you out, and dull your blades to hell. My blades run almost $40 bucks a set and you'll probably hit something you couldn't see in there & ruin em' anyway.

Which brings me to another point. I have a disclaimer in my estimate stating If the lawn is so tall that objects like sprinkler heads, landscape lighting, well pipes etc. are not clearly visible, we are not responsible for damage to such items (or anything they may hit when they come flying out). Cover your butt! You are gonna hit this stuff. I explain we try not too & we aren't asking for a license to be careless but you can't avoid what you can't see."

Should I buy an office for my lawn care business?

When it comes to running the back office of your lawn care business, you may wonder where do most lawn care businesses operate from? Do they run it out of their home or do they buy office space? What about equipment storage? Where do they keep everything at the end of the day? Some lawn care business owners may have a need for an office away from their home but what ever it is you are purchasing, you always have to ask yourself, can I do it for cheaper and save that money for use elsewhere?

A lawn care business owner asked his question about office space on the Gopher Lawn Care Business Forum and got quite a few responses. He wrote "I am new to the lawn care industry and this is just my second summer. Last summer I had 50 residential yards on my schedule and expect a lot more this summer. I was thinking of moving my office out of my basement and purchasing a small office building to look more professional. Do you think this is a good idea? Do most of you operate your office out of your houses? And where do you keep your equipment? Any advice will help me a lot."

One lawn care business owner replied "I have just over 5 acres of property with four buildings on it. I keep my equipment indoors during the winter. In the summer, excavators and tractors almost always stay on job sites. Mowers, blowers, trimmers etc. are parked here at my home at night with the company vehicle.

I used to have daily meetings in the morning here at my home with my staff, however we have moved to a local coffee shop not far from my house. Generally we all talk for 15 to 30 min about the day ahead, issues from the previous day, equipment issues or questions and then head out. The guys are allowed to switch the crew they are on as long as they are trained in each others job. Sometimes I will quickly lay out upcoming jobs in the very near future. To me it's all about team building. I am no better than anyone on the team. On job sites we are all equal, it really works.

On Wednesday evenings we go to an all you can eat sports bar. I generally have one beer with the guys, something to eat and that is about it. The guys are all good and take the work for the coming day very serious. I never once had an employee call in sick or not show last year. I am very proud of the team. Another added benefit of meeting like this in a public place is that I discovered we pick up more business when we met like this. There are generally 12 to 14 of us along with four vehicles at the local coffee shop, so it has been amazing marketing. Local residents quite often come up to me while we are meeting to discuss issues they are having with their property."

A second lawn care business owner said "I built a 12X14 steel building to keep my equipment in last year. I got tired of always loading and unloading so now I just keep the common equipment in the truck and the other stuff like the equipment which is rarely used stays in the shop. I only bring the equipment needed for that day to minimize my loading and unloading times. My office was in a spare room of my house, but now as I am expecting my third child, I gave up the room and have a make shift office in the laundry room."

A third business owner said "personally, I can't justify any additional overhead at this point. I would love to have a store front type office in the future, something that would allow me to offer more than just lawn service. I want to sell anything that one could buy for their yard, lawn furniture, fountains, special nick knacks and other things as well as offering our services.

For the time being, I'm operating out of my apartment. My equipment is stored in an enclosed cargo trailer that is almost always attached to my truck. Any equipment not in use such as snow removal stuff in the summer or mowers and such in winter I store in a storage unit I rent. I also use the storage unit as a shop during the summer months. The equipment storage costs me less than $100 per month."

A fourth business owner said "having an office away from your home will cut into your profits. Don't do it unless you absolutely have too. If looking professional is all you need, there are much easier solutions. A nice web site and a virtual office. Lawn care customers will never be coming to your office anyway.

I run my business out of my home and have my wife answer the phone, handle my mail and messages. I should mention this method is dirt cheap compared to the price of office space and staff. Get your family involved if you have the option. You will feel good about it and they will feel good about it."

How my landscape trailer was stolen.

We learn a lot of great lessons about business and life on the Gopher Lawn Care Business Forum. Some of these lessons stand out more than others. This specific lesson I felt was real important for everyone to read in order to have a head's up about theft of lawn care equipment. The more you know about how thefts occur, the better you can protect yourself from them.

One lawn care business owner wrote us and shared how his landscape trailer, with all his mowers and other equipment was stolen. He said "my business was finally where it was doing great and my week was full. I had just gotten 2 new commercial lawn care clients. I updated all my equipment and had a recently purchased a new enclosed trailer. Life was good until....

Driving back home from a mowing account, my truck broke down and I pulled off on the side of the freeway. I called AAA to get my truck towed. They came out at 4:30 pm to tow the truck and said they couldn't tow the truck and the trailer. AAA only covers towing the truck. I put the coupler lock on the trailer and left it there. Got the truck towed to repair shop and went to U-haul to rent a truck to go get the trailer. When I got back out to where the trailer was at 5:30pm, it was gone. The entire trailer with all my equipment is now gone.

I called the police to see if they may have towed it and they said they didn't. So I filed a theft report with them. After that I called my insurance company. They said I can get some money to replace the trailer and equipment but it will take 4 weeks before everything goes through. 4 weeks!!! I can't wait 4 weeks.

I spent most of the next day calling clients and letting them know what was happening. Now I will have to start my business all over. I don't have the money to go out now and get everything I need to get up and running again.

Whenever I get back going again and I get a new trailer I am going to buy one of those boots to put around the wheel and look into putting a LoJack or something like that on my trailer. This has totally wiped me out.

What lessons did I learn from all this?

I do have insurance however I don't have the coverage I thought I was getting. Lesson #1 if you don't understand all the legal wording in the insurance forms get someone who does to explain it to you.

So basically the insurance has a loss of use coverage and they pay for all equipment under $500.00. However it is more of a reimbursement than a coverage. Basically what I found out was that my choices are to replace all my equipment out of pocket and they will reimburse me after things go through their system or wait until it goes through the system and get money to replace the equipment. The clause in the policy is what is holding me up now.

I now understand if anything is stolen I have to wait a certain amount of time to give law enforcement a chance to recover stolen items. This supposedly helps in fraudulent claims so people don't double there equipment by reporting false thefts. So I do have insurance just not the right kind or the right company.

Lesson #2 I learned was, just because your car insurance company offers business insurance it may not be the best for you. Make sure you know what they are offering and what they cover. It may be a little more expensive to go with a different company but they may have better coverage. I went with my car insurance company because they were in the middle price range. They also gave me a discount because I have my home and cars through them. The bulk discount may not be your best bet.

Make sure you know what insurance you have and don't just go with the cheapest. My insurance company wasn't the cheapest but they were less expensive than others and I already had my cars insured with them. However, their business insurance is lacking. I still like the coverage and service I get with my autos but I will be looking elsewhere for the business insurance once I am up and running again.

Lesson #3 don't leave your trailer on the highway, ever. The towing company said they could have towed my trailer for an additional $55.00 hook up fee and $5.00 a mile. In total, it would have come out to around $130.00 for them to tow it. I thought I would save money by just renting and U-haul to go back and get. The rental only cost me $45.00.

I talked to another guy here in town and he said that he once had to leave his trailer on the road. So he took whatever he could fit in the back of his truck out of the trailer. He then jacked up the trailer and took one of the tires with him also. Not a bad idea since then it can't go anywhere.

The towing company said that anytime you are pulling a trailer and need a tow, make sure you let them know so they will send a flatbed out to get it. Then they can put the truck on the flatbed and tow the trailer behind.

Keep these lessons I learned in mind the next time you are out pulling a trailer and have a break down. They just might save your business."

What's the quickest ways to pick up leaves?

As soon as early September hits, leaves start to fall from the trees. When this happens, customers start getting itchy to have these leaves removed. As a lawn care business owner, your job should be to find ways to minimize the time spent picking up these leaves in order for you to spend the least time on each property while maximizing your profit. But what leaf removal methods are the fastest? That is what one lawn care business owner questioned on the Gopher Lawn Care Business Forum when he wrote "What is the best and most efficient way to pick up leaves? Some of the yards that we maintain have heavy leaf fall. Any ideas on the best way to clean up the yard?"

One lawn care business owner wrote "The one method we use is to blow the leaves onto a tarp and then lift it all into the truck to dispose of. If you don't have that kind of space on your truck or trailer for all those leaves, here is another method. Mulch the leaves up first with your mower and then throw the bag on the lawn mowers and pick them up that way."

Another lawn care business owner said "this is what we do for 95%+ of the yards. However, it does depend on your budget. It can be, to some, an expensive investment however this is how I have grown my company every year and enjoy setting the bar a little higher each year. What I have been doing is selling the client on having their leaves shredded and placed in a neat pile in their yard. It is working beyond my dreams.

The most profitable and efficient way I have found to do this is by having two lawn vacs running behind my tractors from sunrise to sunset. If due to the property, we can't use the vac shredder, I pass on the job as I am not interested in blowing and hauling.

I blow the leaves away from fences, out of mulch beds etc, drive over them with one of the tractors which has high lift mulching blades (twice). After explaining to the customer, the high nutrient value of the shredded leaves, the clients tend to want the mulched leaves left on the lawn, we also offer an organic spray to decompose them faster. If you go over them twice they are really fine, in other cases we pull a sweeper and leave them in a pile.

If you get into offering organic sprays, you are looking at a 300% ++ markup and trust me you will get it. We started offering these spray services in early spring and have since spray over 169 clients. At every leaf job we upsell an organic compost accelerator and make a killing off of it.

Why simply profit from removing the leaves, when you can profit further with these upsells and not have to haul away and dispose of them!"

A third lawn care business owner said "what I do is blow all leaves out of the landscapes and hard surfaces and then run a bagger on my mower until the leaves completely fill it. Then I run over the rest of the lawn with the full bag acting as a mulching block which will chop up the rest of the leaves into dust and tiny pieces. I empty the bag when it is full and go over the lawn in a different direction. It fills up much less with the mulched up pieces than it does with full sized leaves. I empty as it fills this time around."

These great ideas will give you more options when it comes to offering leaf cleanup services this fall and more ways to profit!

Pressure washing services you can add on.

A great service you can perform when you can't mow due to rain, is pressure washing. Getting started offering this service shouldn't be that difficult and it can help your business expand outwards. One lawn care business owner was looking to get into power washing and had a few questions about getting started that he posted on the Gopher Lawn Care Business Forum.

He wrote "I want to start getting into offering concrete pressure washing services. I think by adding a service to pressure wash driveways I will be able to make more profits out of my current customer base but I am not sure on a few issues. Can anyone tell me what too charge per sq ft? I'm also considering purchasing a mechanical concrete cleaner. Is this a good idea?"

Another lawn care business owner shared "You can offer many services when you have a pressure washer. I offer to clean driveways, sidewalks, whole houses (from grass to soffit), pool areas, screen enclosures and patios (wood or concrete).

A great tool that helps out a lot when doing the driveway is a buffing machine or a surface cleaner. It cuts down on the time spent on site, makes the job so much easier, and in the end makes it more profitable. If you use chlorine to help clean the area, buy it from a pool supply store in the 2.5 gallon container. Dilute it with water when you add it to your sprayer to pre-treat the area you are about to clean.

The costs I charge are as followed"

1. Driveway / Sidewalk $.10 per sq. foot (Avg. size DW 12' x 100' SW 4' x 50') Generally most of the jobs I do are about the

same size. I don't measure all the time and charge $150 per job.

2. Whole House $150 - $200 per house (grass to soffit) Avg. house 2,000 – 3,000 sq. ft.

3. Pool Area / Screen Enclosure, depending on size, $75 pool area $150 pool & enclosure. If there is mildew on the aluminum enclosure that requires scrubbing and getting on a ladder, then I add $50- $75 more to the cost.

4. Patios / Decks Concrete or Wood 10'x 50' size $50 - $75

I hope this helps you out. My prices may be high or low in your area but it works for me where I am at and I make a good profit for the amount of time I spend doing these jobs.

A surface cleaner can be used on any hard flat surface. You just need to know your machine and the surface being cleaned and adjust accordingly. DO NOT use this on wood unless you want to do a lot of sanding. Asphalt is softer than concrete so it requires less pressure.

It has multiple spray nozzles underneath that rotate under a shroud that cleans faster than you can with a wand. I have used them to clean sidewalks where it took me 1 minute and 40 seconds to clean which would have taken 15 to 30 minutes with a wand. With the surface cleaner you can clean an average sized driveway in under 30 minutes. After you clean, all you do is rinse the water off the surface and you are done. That is unless you have a recovery system that negates the need to rinse because it picks up all the dirty water. It is kind of like a mower blade with a spray nozzle at each end of the blade spinning at a high rate of speed.

At another job site I cleaned a strip mall, it had 18,000 sq ft of concrete. I used one surface cleaner and had a man rinsing behind me and removing the gum. It took about 5 1/2 hours… To me that's pretty fast! On this job it equaled out to be just over $200 an hour.

For those that are considering adding pressure washing, you should see a demo of the equipment in use at a local dealer before you buy."

SALES

A great lawn care business upsell service to offer.

Every lawn care business owner is always looking for more services to offer as upsells. There is plenty of money to be made out there and customers are willing to pay you if you are able to suggest to them a service they could use. How about this idea a member of the Gopher Lawn Care Business Forum offers and makes money at.

He wrote "I am always thinking of ways to add services to help out my clients and add more money to the bottom line. We all add on services like gutter cleaning, tree/shrub trimming, pressure washing, irrigation repairs/cleanouts, handyman service and the one I like the most is dog walking. LOL

My new service I will be offering is a Vent Clean Out service for the dryer in your house. You ask what is this and how did I come across this one? I'll tell you.

My friend was having problems with his dryer not drying fast enough or heating up to the proper temperature to dry the clothes. He thought the dryer was old and broken. So he and his wife went out and bought a new one and of course they had to buy the matching washer. They gave the old one to their daughter to use as a back up. When the men came to install and remove the old units they asked my friend when was the last time they had cleaned out the dryer vent? You know the one that goes into the wall and either out to the roof or outside wall? They said,'I clean out the snake looking aluminum one often.' He said no the one that releases the lint and hot air outside. They said never.

Well to make a long story short they cleaned out the piping and vent and had a shopping bag filled with lint. They said over time this may cause a fire or burn out the dryer from overheating.

After cleaning the vent, everything worked fine. At the daughters house the mother told her about this and her husband cleaned his out and tried the dryer out and it worked perfectly and heated up nice and hot. Wasted money for them, is now a New Service to Offer for me.

They told me about this and I went home and cleaned out my vent and duck work. My dryer wasn't all that hot either. After the clean out, my dryer was like new. I had about a half of bag of lint. My neighbor saw me on my roof cleaning out the vent and asked what I was doing and I told him. He asked me to clean his and paid me $15.00 for about 15 minutes of work. Then a light bulb went off in my head!! Here is a service I can offer to my clients. It's a no brainer. Everyone is concerned about losing their home to fire or theft.

So this is what I did.

1. I went on the roof (or wall vent) and cleaned it out.
2. Went inside and moved the dryer and removed the snake like aluminum tube and cleaned it out.
3. Took my wet vac and reversed it to blow out the vent leading to the roof. If you don't have a wet vac, use you back pack blower. The blower will leave a smell of exhaust. (My neighbor said it looked like it was snowing) I did this several times to ensure that everything was clean.
4. Vacuumed up the dust or lint in the room.
5. Reattached everything and turned on the dryer to make sure it worked properly. A Okay.

The end result was the customer was happy, I am happy and now I have more money in my pocket.

You may not be too sure that this really goes with lawn care but, when you are at a customer's house, look at it from the road, look for things you can do to make more money and make the customer's life easier. Sales and money will follow."

When should you offer discounts on lawn care?

When should you offer lawn care customers, a discount? Should they be offered a discount if they pay in cash? Or what about a discount to seal the deal if they are on the fence? Do discounts help or do they make you look desperate?

Here is what one lawn care business owner wrote. "Should I offer a certain % discount when a customer wants to pay in cash? But then what should I do when the work is all done and then the customer wants to write a check? Or when I have a contract that states 1/2 the money up front and the rest of it upon completion only to find out that when I get done with the job and the customer decides they want to send me a check? I'm thinking about tacking on something a little extra for those customers who want to try too screw me over."

One lawn care business owner suggested "when I start any landscaping project over $300 I write an estimate/contract and in that contract it clearly states that before I start the project I am to be paid half upfront and when I finish the other half I get paid the rest. Then we both sign it.

Normally I don't have a problem with customers paying but if they want to push off the final part for a week or so by sending me a check through the mail which wasn't part of the deal, they will then have to pay a late fee which is in the contract as well. I point this out to them when the problem arises and it tends to resolve the issue."

A second business owner said "people sometimes ask me If I prefer to be paid with cash or by check. Some even ask if there is a discount. When this happens, I just explain that it doesn't really matter to me. No matter how I get paid, I claim the money in my taxes.

Besides it being the right thing to do, I want to point out a reason how claiming or not claiming money can effect you in the future, in a way you might not initially think of. Right now I have 2 kids, a little boy and a little girl in the same bedroom. I can only get away with that for a few more years until they get a little older. Then I will want/need a bigger house, possibly in the next year or so. I have pretty good credit now which is fine, but if I can't show the actual income I make, I won't qualify for the loan I want. So I claim everything.

Customers at times need to understand that I do run my business as I should. I pay insurance and taxes. I offer the best prices I can with all that in mind and my price is what it is. I don't care how they pay as long as they do."

A third business owner said "first off, I am in business to make money. Not to work for less than I know the job is worth. With that said, the only discounts I offer are for annual contracts paid in advance for the year, instead of pay as you go. But on the other hand I do have this to say, perception is 90% of the yes factor from a potential customer. By this I mean, say I have a job to re-mulch a flower bed and I do my figures and come up with the price I would do it for, that covers all my costs. For instance, if my bid totals $150.00 then I will add an additional 20% = $30.00 to the bid. This bid now totals $180.00.

Now when you present the bid price to your customer, you will get 1 of 4 basic responses.

1) Good for you, they say ok when can you start.

2) We will let you know. This tells you they think it's too much. But if you respond with 'hey mr/mrs customer I really want this

job, if I took 10% off, would we have a deal?' Remember you added 20% above the real quote you came up with. You could probably cut even a little more and still be good.

3) The customer says 'thanks but no thanks.' In this situation, refer to rule #2

4) Can you do any better on the price? Yes you can! Refer back to rule #2.

All people want is to feel like they are getting a good deal. Response #1 is always great to hear but that happens maybe 1 out of 5 times. Normally I get response #2 or #4 which is fine with me. That shows me they are interested in my service and I have the chance to make a higher profit. My normal is approximately a 25% profit margin in a quote. Then I add the 20% on top of that. I usually get 10% to 15% of that additional markup.

I have found that most people I get calls from don't get many bids. They just use the 1st one they feel can do the job and who makes them feel like they are getting a good deal."

How to promote your lawn care business without coming across as pushy.

Everyone hates pushy people. And pushy sales people are even more hated. So what is a lawn care business owner to do when they want to promote their business but not come across as being pushy? That is a great topic that came up on the Gopher Lawn Care Business Forum, when a business owner shared with us some of his tips.

He wrote "I just recently moved and had to start up my lawn care business in a new area from scratch. I had previously started my lawn care business while I was in high school with a friend. Regardless of if you are a new owner or a veteran, you gotta get the word out about your business. One of the things I do is to make sure everyone that I know, knows that I have a lawn care business. Word of mouth is a great marketing tool. The more people who know you are in business, the more opportunity you have to sell your services.

It is difficult to tell everyone without someone thinking you are just trying to push your business on them and make them feel that they are obligated to use you. To get around this, what I usually do is just more or less ask questions. For instance I will ask a homeowner 'who currently cuts your lawn? Who installed that wall? It looks great.' I always like to compliment what they have or what they are getting. But then I always throw in the 'well next time you need some work done I am in the business, here is my card, please call me.' Depending on how well you you interact with the person, you can get them to market your business as well.

To be successful, you really gotta focus on not pushing what you do, but instead, engage the potential customer in a conversation.

Talk to them about issues you may see about their yard or ask them if they have had any problems lately with their landscaping. Is there anything on their landscaping wish list? The more you engage them the better your chances are of making a sale and then later getting that customer to talk about you to their friends."

How a few calls landed some big jobs.

A great way to get jobs is to keep your eyes open when you are out driving around town. If you see a site that seems like it could use your services, don't wait for the land owner to come to you, go to them. That is exactly what this lawn care business owner did and as soon as he decided to be proactive, he found a lot more work. He shared his story with us on the Gopher Lawn Care Business Forum.

He wrote "I have a huge cemetery right next to my house. It is also right next to a school. Well in the winter months, I noticed that the sidewalks were not taken care of at all and the kids were walking in the street to avoid the sidewalk. The sidewalk is long too, about 1 mile if you add it up the total length.

Since I offer snow removal services in the winter, I thought this would be a great bid to land so I politely called them to ask if my company could take care of the sidewalk for them. They initially told me they were not responsible for the sidewalks and therefore did not need for me to remove the snow. I thought they were mistaken and decided investigate this further. I then called the city to see who is responsible for these sidewalks and they told me the cemetery was!

After that I called the cemetery back and very nicely explained what the township told me and if they need any help with anything, grass, plowing, etc...to call me. Once they were told that they were indeed responsible for keeping the sidewalks clear and that they were a hazard for the school kids they hired me to keep the sidewalks clear of snow! It is a huge job @ $1.00 per minute per man, plus $.25 per pound of salt used! All of this from making three phone calls! I also might be getting more work from them in the summer as well.

You really have to be proactive. I absolutely benefit from living close by. People tend to feel more comfortable hiring locally and there is hardly any traveling expense to perform this job."

That is an awesome story! I think that would make for some great marketing material. Telling the potential customer they could be fined for not cleaning their sidewalks of snow and then offering to do it for them!

"But wait my success doesn't end there. After finding this information out, I did a little more digging. By talking to people at the town hall I figured out the township has this list of contractors. When the city inspectors notice something wrong while doing a general inspection of a house or building, the home owners has to use a contractor from this list to make repairs! I learned it is an easy process and I think it will generate tons of business for me.

Here is how I did it:

I called the city and asked them how to get on that list of contractors. All you need is your proof of insurance, and your company's employee identification number.

In my town there was no 'landscaping' category, but there were other services like plumbing, electrical, structural, masonry, etc. In the past, I have done a some masonry jobs and it's the one most closely related to landscaping so I decided to get a masonry license. It cost me $175.00 and there wasn't any test!

Some of the additional benefits to being on this list are, if there is anyone who has not kept their sidewalks cleared of snow, the property owner gets a fine from the city and this list of contractors. They also can be fined if the grass is over 6 inches as well. So since my company is the only one on the list that has a business name which includes landscaping in it I'll most likely be getting a lot more calls.

I suggest you contact your town hall and get on the list in your area too."

Getting your foot in the door.

Coming up with a game plan and marketing strategy for your lawn care business can be tough. A member of the Gopher Lawn Care Business Forum shared with us his frustrations when trying to figure out a way to get his foot in the door with potential customers that live near him yet are serviced by another lawn care business.

He wrote "I have been staying up for days thinking about my spring lawn care marketing plan. I'm having some serious anxieties here. I have lawns all over the city, but I have built up one nice street all to myself.

The problem is, I want the clients other companies have that are literally RIGHT beside me. There are about 12 lawns I want to grab, all of them small to average in size. I have asked around and found out these potential customers are paying $32.00 more than my service per month. I need a strategy to get them to sign up with me. I really want these clients! I know I can make a lot more from offering them many upsells.

What I have come up with so far is to give them my business card in March/April with my estimate already written on the back. Then I will personally visit them the week after. Maybe I can attach a note to the card mentioning the perks my service offers?

Perks, hmmm.

I can mention, I'm a neighbor to all of them and they will receive top priority. These customers will be my baby. If they pay $75.00+ for mowing, they will receive a free garden weeding once per month.

Maybe I'll even throw in a free mowing…

HMMMM. I need these customers.

If I get them I will have 20 customers no more than half a mile away from home! Can anyone help me out with this?"

Another lawn care business owner said "I think what you have so far is a good plan. You should proceed with it and see what happens.

When it comes to lawn mowing, trimming, weeding, what I have found customers tend to go allow with the phrase 'better the devil you know than the one you don't.' That can be the attitude of a prospective customer. If they have been with their lawn company for X years and are satisfied with the service, it can be almost impossible to get them to switch.

The one way I found you can get your foot in the door is to offer a service that will benefit the client that the current lawn care provider does not. In my case it is organic spraying with a now proven track record. It took me time to build the references I needed to help sell it, but now that I have them. With those references this year should be even more amazing than last.

To cut time spraying, I doubt we will use the backpack sprayers very often if at all. I added tow and 3 pt hitch sprayers to every piece of equipment we own. I can now get into some really, really tight spots without ever getting off a tractor and if needed, I have a 26 foot wand that can be used as well. It should be a lot easier on the staff. Back pack spraying on larger lawns is brutal. Also, if you find you need to spray in the rain, which we generally have to do, you want in and out pretty quick.

Before you sink a lot of coin into this venture, test the waters first and advertise the service. You can get the product within a few days and a sprayer the same day. Keep your overhead low to ensure there is demand.

My advertisements are somewhat short and sweet. They direct the customer or prospect to my website. I have found it would simply be too expensive to have all the information printed.

Points to highlight in your ad:

Certified Organic Lawn Care Products - All food grade being children and pet safe

We can cure - Brown Patch, any insect or bug, Clay or Compacted soils. If you want a golf course looking lawn you need to check us out, over 170 references available."

How I found commercial lawn care property bids in my area.

Finding commercial lawn care bids is not as difficult as you may think. Most times it comes down to picking up the phone and finding who to talk to or simply visiting the establishment and asking a few questions. That is what a member of the Gopher Lawn Care Business Forum did when he found a fast food business who needed a lawn care bid for five of their properties.

He wrote "I am going to be bidding on 5 fast food chain locations. The work to be done is mowing, trimming, and blowing off the parking lot and walkways of grass clippings, once per week. Each site is between 1.3 - 1.6 acres. I am estimating that each site will have about 30 min. of mowing.

To find this job, what I did was call up the restaurant, introduced myself, first name, and name of my business. Then I told them that I would like to put a bid in for their lawn care this season and asked who I could speak with about that. They gave me the name and number of their franchise owner and I gave him a call and left a similar message.

He called back that same day and said that he would be interested in getting quotes. An added bonus for me is that he said he owned four other locations and said he would like bids on those also.

Being new to commercial lawn care, this is how I have come to have the chance to submit all of my quotes. I literally drove around the areas that I was interested in. I wrote down information about the locations. When I got home later, I looked them up in the phone book or got the number off their signs. After that I started making calls. By doing that, I am now bidding on a church (6-7 acres), those 5 fast food locations, another fast food location, and a small hotel. I was nervous at first, but everyone has been very polite. If they do their own lawn care, I thank them for their time, leave my card and let them know if they are ever interested to please feel free to call.

For the fast food jobs, I figure it would take about 30 minutes of mowing for each site. Trimming, I am estimating about 10-15 minutes (most of the trees are mulched around). I think that by myself I could be in and out of there in about an hour. My payment terms are within 15 days of the invoice, billed the first of each month. I plan to stop mowing if payments are not received though. I learned a tough collection lesson last year and am still trying to collect $400 from a previous customer.

I measured the mulch beds and am quoting, they would need another 1"-2" of mulch installed. I calculated the amount of mulch needed by figuring the total sq. ft. of each bed and dividing that by 165 to get how many yards I would need. Then I calculated how much to charge for this by doubling the price I pay for mulch to cover the time spent laying it.

As far as bush trimming I quote them per bush. Example: bushes knee high or less = $3.00 per bush. Knee to waist high = $5.00 per bush. Waist and higher = $10-$20 per bush. I am going with that method until I can get a better idea of how long it takes me to trim them.

So, all in all I will bid a price for mowing, trimming and blowing, then a price for bush trimming (each occurrence) and another price for mulch. I did not ask about the trash removal from the parking lot, but I will see if they are interested in that service too. I would pick up any trash if it were on the lawns. But I can already tell there will probably be a high occurrence of this so I need to account for the time to perform this in the bid as well."

Another lawn care business owner suggested "your bid should

include: mulching twice a year, bush trimming once a month, weeding twice a month, leaf pick up twice in the fall and litter clean-up every week. Make it a package deal, find out how much it would cost them for a full year and divide it by twelve and put them on a twelve month paying schedule so you get paid every month for a full year. Make sure you continue to do stuff like leaf clean up, litter pick up and stuff like that even through the winter months."

How to land restaurants and hotels as lawn care clients.

Any time I hear a great story about how a lawn care business owner landed some commercial accounts, I like to share the story with everyone to help you see how others do it. We all need to hear stories and experiences from others in order to broaden our horizons. This story came to us through the Gopher Lawn Care Business Forum where a member shared with us how he landed 4 hotels, 2 restaurants and 47 residential lawn care accounts. Look at the way he did it and compare his operation with yours. Are there areas in your business you could improve upon?

He wrote "I restarted my lawn service last year. I used to have about 12 yards in high school, but girls and the beach were way more important than cutting grass and my business failed because of it. After that experience I worked for a landscaping company through college. Later I worked as a regional manager for a cellular dealer for 9 years until that got old.

During that time I save up some money and left that line of work to restart my lawn care business. From the advice that I got on this site, I now have 4 hotels, 2 restaurants and 47 residential.

The 2 restaurants I got by just going up to the managers and asking them who is doing there lawn service (because it looked awful) and they said basically they didn't have anyone. I gave them a price and showed up the next day and started edging and mowing. It was that simple! So as you drive around town, keep your eyes open and don't be afraid to walk in the door and introduce yourself!

I got the 4 hotels from the signs on my landscaping truck & trailer. The property manager from all 4 hotels called to get an estimate for his house. While speaking with him I told him I provide commercial lawn services as well. From there, he told me what he did and said he wasn't happy with his current landscaping company....so for about a month we went back and forth on prices and the only way to close the deal was to throw in his house lawn service for free in the whole deal (his yard only takes 25 mins to edge and mow..no big lost there), so I said yes and sealed the deal.

I made the graphics for my trailer on my own computer and emailed them to a local sign & banner company. We decided to put them on the side of my truck for people to see when my trailer was off. I have the same sign on the back of my trailer also! This is such a simple step, every lawn care business should be doing this.

Next season this hotel company is opening up 2 more hotels and I also got the contract to mow those properties as well. Another marketing angle I was able to work is reaching out to all the employees at each hotel. I was able to put up a flyer in their break room and send a flyer home with their pay check! Example: ABC Hotel employee get a 10% discount on yard service! This discount to his employees made the manager look good and also got me more local residential lawn care accounts.

When I need more residential lawn care customers, I knock on doors that need bushes, mulching, mowing and edging done. This works great. While I am there, I will offer my weekly or bi-weekly lawn care services. Once I get them as customers I ask for and start getting referrals."

Getting municipal government lawn care accounts.

When you think of the different kind of customer to target in your business plan, you probably think of the usual residential and commercial customers. But what if you expanded your horizon and thought a little outside the box. Could you provide lawn care service to your local municipal government? Would they be a great contact to reach out and get more jobs? From what a member of the Gopher Lawn Care Business Forum said, reaching out to your local municipal government, is a great way to get and stay busy cutting lawns.

One business owner wrote "my husband and I started our lawn care service a little over a year ago and we've been able to obtain some lawn care accounts including a few larger accounts through our local municipal government.

From what I have learned through my dealings with the local government, persistence and timing pays off. We never gave up and kept presenting proposals to the municipalities. As we did this, we found that apparently a couple of them were having issues with their current lawn care contractor's work so we were given a chance.

So not only did we find that there was plenty of local government property to mow and maintain, there were also a lot of programs we could get involved with that paid well. For instance, one of the municipalities we found has a vacant home program in which the municipality maintains the lawns of the vacant homes when the owners won't so they contract that work out. Another municipality has a senior grass cutting program that they contract the work out to as well.

So in the end, we found it pays to contact your local government and get your business on the list of contractors that can perform these services. You may be surprised at how much work you get from making such local contacts."

In Conclusion

Starting a lawn care business is a great way to harness your entrepreneurial spirit and make money. After reading this book you should be well ahead of your local start up competitors. While they are out there fumbling around trying to figure out what works and what doesn't, you will be more confident to push forwards. You will also have a better understanding of how to interact with your lawn care customers and grow. Keep yourself learning and investigating the lessons needed to continue your growth. I know you can do it!

Until the next time we meet, always remember to dream it, build it, Gopher it!

Sincerely,
Steve

CPSIA information can be obtained at www.ICGtesting.com
Printed in the USA
LVOW06s2202050314

376244LV00003B/131/P